Green Book

Critical Thinking with Literature

Reading • Writing • Communicating

by
Dorothy Kauffman, Ph.D.
University of Maryland

ISBN 0-8454-2455-6

CONTINENTAL PRESS
Elizabethtown, PA 17022

Credits

Cover Design and Art Direction: Kirchoff/Wohlberg, Inc.

Interior Design: Kevin Miller

Illustration: Pages 6, 7, 37, 44, 54, 59, 80, 85, 88, 96, 107, V. Carlin Verreaux; Pages 8–10, Kristen Nettleton Goeters; Pages 15–18, Kathleen Howell; Pages 22, 30, 35, 36, 61, 63, 73, 107, Margaret Sanfilippo; Pages 23–26, Ron Himler; Pages 31–33, Pat Traub; Pages 38–40, Arvis Stewart; Pages 46–49, Leonard Jenkins; Pages 55–57, Christa Kieffer; Page 62, Floyd Cooper; Pages 67–69, Gail Piazza; Pages 74–77, Esther Baran; Pages 82–83, Al Fiorentino; Page 87, Jim McConnell; Pages 89–91, Tom Leonard; Page 97, Lou Vaccaro; Pages 101–103, Julie Ecklund; Pages 108–110, Betsy Day

Photography: Page 5, Robert E. Kauffman

Acknowledgments

Every effort has been made to trace the ownership of all copyrighted material and to secure the necessary permissions to reprint these selections. In the event of any question arising as to the use of any material, the editor and the publisher, while expressing regret for any inadvertent error, will be happy to make the necessary correction in future printings. Grateful acknowledgment is made to the following for permission to reprint the copyrighted material listed below:

Excerpt pp. 22–24 from MISCHLING, SECOND DEGREE by Ilse Koehn. Copyright © 1977 by Ilse Koehn. Reprinted by permission of Greenwillow Books (A Division of William Morrow and Company, Inc.).

PETER PAN by J. M. Barrie (Charles Scribner's Sons, New York, 1911). Reprinted by permission of Macmillan Publishing Company.

Excerpt from THUNDER AT GETTYSBURG by Patricia Lee Gauch, copyright © 1975 by Patricia Lee Gauch. Reprinted by permission of the author.

Pages 1–3 from THE CRY OF THE CROW by Jean Craighead George. Copyright © 1980 by Jean Craighead George. Reprinted by permission of Harper & Row, Publishers, Inc.

"How the Dragon Lost His Tail" reprinted by permission of G. P. Putnam's Sons from *Tales from a Taiwan Kitchen* by Cora Cheney, copyright © 1976 by Cora Cheney.

From LOST STAR: The Story of Amelia Earhart by Patricia Lauber. Copyright © 1988. Reprinted by permission of Scholastic Inc.

THE LION, THE WITCH AND THE WARDROBE by C. S. Lewis. Copyright © 1965. Reprinted by permission of William Collins Sons & Co. Ltd.

"Foul Shot" by Edwin A. Hoey. Special permission granted by **READ** magazine, published by Field Publications. Copyright © 1962 by Field Publications.

From *Mama's Going to Buy You a Mockingbird* by Jean Little. Copyright © Jean Little, 1984. Reprinted by permission of Penguin Books Canada Limited.

"Time" from THE COW-TAIL SWITCH AND OTHER WEST AFRICAN STORIES by Harold Courlander and George Herzog. Copyright 1947 and renewed 1975 by Harold Courlander. Reprinted by permission of Henry Holt and Company, Inc.

Reprinted with permission of Macmillan Publishing Company from THE GREAT GRADEPOINT MYSTERY by Barbara Bartholomew. Copyright © 1983 by Cloverdale Press.

"It was a stormy night..." from MIND YOUR OWN BUSINESS by Michael Rosen, copyright © 1974. Reprinted by permission of André Deutsch Ltd.

From STREAMS TO THE RIVER, RIVERS TO THE SEA by Scott O'Dell. Copyright © 1986 by Scott O'Dell. Reprinted by permission of Houghton Mifflin Company.

"How Many Donkeys?" from *Once the Hodja* by Alice Geer Kelsey (David McKay Company, Inc., 1968).

CONTENTS

A Note to You 5

Unit One: Sounds of Danger 6

Mischling, Second Degree: My Childhood in Nazi Germany 7
by Ilse Koehn

Peter Pan 14
by J. M. Barrie

Thunder at Gettysburg 22
by Patricia Lee Gauch

The Cry of the Crow 30
by Jean Craighead George

"How the Dragon Lost His Tail" 37
by Cora Cheney

Unit Two: A Matter of Time 44

Lost Star: The Story of Amelia Earhart 45
by Patricia Lauber

The Lion, the Witch and the Wardrobe 53
by C. S. Lewis

"Foul Shot" 61
by Edwin A. Hoey

Mama's Going to Buy You a Mockingbird 66
by Jean Little

"Time" 73
by Harold Courlander and George Herzog

Unit Three: Cut It Out! 80

"Where Did You Get Those Jeans?" 81
by Dotti Kauffman

The Great Gradepoint Mystery 87
by Barbara Bartholomew

"It was a stormy night" 96
by Michael Rosen

Streams to the River, Rivers to the Sea 100
by Scott O'Dell

"How Many Donkeys?" 107
by Alice Geer Kelsey

Dear Friend,

Because you read the title and looked at the cover of this book, you probably think it's a reading book. Well, you're right!

In this book, you will find a lot of different stories and some activities to do after you've finished reading them. In choosing the stories, I looked for subjects and writing styles that kids I know would find interesting and fun to read. When I wrote the activities, I tried to find ways to help you think about the story. I know that sometimes after you read a story, you just fill in the blanks and close the book. I don't want that to happen here, so I talk directly to you in some of the activities. I might give you clues and ideas for an activity or even a sample to start you off. This way, you and I can work together.

By now, you might be wondering what kind of person wrote this book. I like to do a lot of things. I like to read and write. I like to cook, but I hate to clean up. I like to go barefoot, and I like to wear boots. And if I don't like doing something, I put it off till it can't wait any longer. These are just a few things that tell the kind of person I am. Now here's a picture of me and my two cats to show you what I look like.

Happy reading,

Dotti

SOUNDS OF DANGER

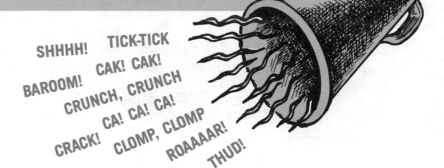

SHHHH! TICK-TICK
BAROOM! CAK! CAK!
CRUNCH, CRUNCH
CA! CA! CA!
CRACK! CLOMP, CLOMP
ROAAAAR!
THUD!

What danger could each sound on the right signal? Read the sounds, and then read the titles listed below. Choose two sounds of danger to go with each title.

Titles	Sounds of Danger
1. *Mischling, Second Degree: My Childhood in Nazi Germany*	_____ _____
2. *Peter Pan*	_____ _____
3. "Thunder at Gettysburg"	_____ _____
4. *The Cry of the Crow*	_____ _____
5. "How the Dragon Lost His Tail"	_____ _____

OK, now listen for the rustle of turning pages as you enter this unit. What SOUNDS OF DANGER do the stories really present? Were your choices correct? Let's go find out!

Getting Ready to Read

1. Gaze into Madame Zizi's crystal ball at the right. What predictions might it make for the characters listed below? Write two predictions for each one.

A millionaire _____

_____

A politician _____

_____

A person your age living in Nazi Germany in 1937 _____

_____

2. Now think about that last character above. Choose three sounds that might alert that person to danger. List your three sounds below and what could cause each one.

Sound of Danger	Source
☆ _____	☆ _____
☆ _____	☆ _____
☆ _____	☆ _____

Reading

Even today the words *Hitler* and *Nazis* stir up ugly images of human torture and death. The story you're going to read is about growing up in Nazi Germany. Because her great-grandparents were Jewish, Ilse Koehn was known as a "Mischling, Second Degree." What sounds of danger would Ilse have grown to fear? To find out, read Ilse's story. Answer the questions in the margin while you read.

Mischling, Second Degree

My Childhood in Nazi Germany

by Ilse Koehn

It was a nice afternoon. Oma and I were reading when there was a sharp knock at the door, instantly followed by a staccato of louder, authoritative pounding. When I opened the door, I faced what seemed to be a gray wall moving toward me. I had the nightmare feeling that it would come close, closer, and crush me.

It consisted of two huge women dressed in long, identical gray coats with big black handbags and laced boots. Ugly, flat, black boots. They had pallid faces, and their hair was tied back so tightly they seemed bald.

"That must be her!" said one, pulling me up against her enormous body by one of my pigtails. She held it painfully tight, using her other hand to part the hair on my head this way and that. Then she released me with a push that made me stumble backward against Oma.

"At least she doesn't have lice!" she declared. "Is this the child?" she demanded of Oma as if she had caught her with stolen goods. But she did not wait for an answer. "We are social workers," she continued in that same tone. "We've come to see whether the child is being properly cared for. Where does she sleep?"

What sounds disturbed the afternoon?

Why had the women come?

What were the women doing?

Oma pointed, and both women went over to my bed, lifted the cover, looked under the pillow, the mattress, pulled the bedclothes apart and left them.

"Where do you keep her things?"

Again Oma just pointed and immediately they descended on the chest of drawers. They burrowed into my underwear, my scarves and mittens and my small belongings. Having made a mess here, too, they stomped over to the closet, and in passing hit Oma with one of their monstrous bags. There was no apology. How they yanked at the clothes, all but ripping them off their hangers! And not only mine, but Oma's and Vati's as well.

Shoulder to shoulder, they steamrollered their way to the kitchen. "Is this where you prepare her meals?"

Oma said nothing, watched as they went through cupboards and looked into drawers and pots.

What were they looking for? Why didn't Oma tell them to leave? But now apparently they were finished. They walked out of the door, barked, "You will hear from us!" and, still side by side, marched down the stairs. I closed the door, tried to look at Oma, but she hid her face as she put things back in order.

What did Ilse find out?

Not long after their visit, a letter arrived from my grandparents. Without comment, Oma quickly dropped it into her drawer. This heightened my curiosity, since she normally showed me what little mail she got. When, a few days later, she went to see a neighbor, I did what I knew I should not do. I opened the drawer. In the letter my grandparents informed Oma that they had applied to the state to be given custody of me. My heart began to pound. I knew it would mean living in Luebars.

Soon afterward Vati told me about it. "It will only be temporary," he said. "I'm still fighting to get you back." As if I was already gone! Pushed around like a ping-pong ball, and how can you cry and be miserable because you've been told to live with your mother, whom you love? "A few days," "a little while," "only temporary"! Didn't I belong anywhere anymore?

"You will soon be going to high school here in Hermsdorf," Vati said, as if this solved everything.

Thinking About What You Read

What did you find out?

1. What sounds of danger were mentioned or suggested in the story? Add three more to the list I've started for you.

☆ *a sharp knock at the door* _____

☆ _____

☆ _____

☆ _____

2. When the two visitors spoke, what tone of voice did they use? What was the volume? How do you know?

_____

_____

_____

3. What words could you use to describe how the main characters felt as the two women swept through the rooms?

☆ _____   ☆ _____

☆ _____   ☆ _____

4. Oma received a letter from Ilse's grandparents, but she hid it right away. Why do you think she did that?

_____

_____

5. While Oma was out, Ilse opened Oma's drawer and read the letter. Ilse knew that she was doing something she shouldn't do. Have you ever done something like that? How did you feel when you did it? Describe what you did and how you felt about it.

_____

_____

_____

_____

11

How did the author help you read the story?

When Ms. Koehn described the visit of the two women, she wanted her readers to hear, see, and feel exactly what the characters heard, saw, and felt. Her description was incredibly real and powerful. But just what made it so powerful? Well, Ms. Koehn chose her words very carefully. She used **vivid vocabulary** rather than weak, general words. Vivid vocabulary is made up of nouns, verbs, adjectives, and adverbs that make writing come alive for readers. Let's look at how the author used it.

1. Read through the story again quickly. Find three adjectives that Ms. Koehn used instead of the weak word *big*. Write them on the lines below.

_____   _____   _____

2. I'm sure you found the words I meant! Now let's look at the story again. Find three verbs that the author used instead of the weak word *walked*. Write the verbs on the lines below.

_____   _____   _____

3. OK, let's do this one more time. This time, read the weak, general terms listed below on the left. Then reread the story to find the vivid terms the author used. Write the vivid terms on the right. (HINT: Be sure to find *two* words to replace *said!*)

Weak, General Terms	Vivid Vocabulary
dream	_____
hair	_____
very	_____
said	_____
	_____
asked	_____
went down	_____
dug	_____
pulled	_____

4. Now, just why is it better to use vivid terms than weak or general ones?

_____

_____

_____

How can you use vivid vocabulary to make your writing alive and powerful?

Imagine that you are Ilse or Oma. The two huge women in gray have just left. If you kept a daily journal, how would you describe this day? What would you say about the two women and their visit? Write your journal entry below. Try to use as many vivid words as you can. When you are done, go back and reread your entry. Cross out any weak, general words and replace them with stronger, more vivid ones.

_____

_____

_____

_____

_____

_____

_____

_____

_____

_____

_____

_____

_____

_____

_____

_____

_____

_____

_____

_____

_____

_____

Getting Ready to Read

My guess is that you already know the story of Peter Pan. You remember how one night Peter and the fairy Tinker Bell fly into the nursery where Wendy, John, and Michael are sleeping. When the children wake up, Peter teaches them to fly. They fly "second to the right and straight on till morning" to reach Never-Never Land, the island where the lost boys, Captain Hook, the pirates, the Indians, and the crocodile all live. You remember, too, that the crocodile wants to eat all of Captain Hook now that he's had a taste of his hand. The crocodile still ticks because it swallowed a clock, too. All of these characters live in constant fear of one another.

1. Now think about the fears of the lost boys and the others. When you are afraid, what happens to your body? Make a list of your body's reactions to fear. I've started the list for you with one of my own. (HINT: What happens to your stomach? Your feet? Your heart?)

☆ *My hands get sweaty.*

☆ _____

☆ _____

☆ _____

2. Suppose you were captured by Captain Hook and taken prisoner on his pirate ship, the *Jolly Roger*. There is no hope for your rescue, for Hook says he has poisoned Peter Pan. You are doomed! What is the worst danger you face from Hook and his crew?

_____

_____

3. What three sounds might alert you to the danger that faces you?

☆ _____

☆ _____

☆ _____

Reading

Uh-oh, you're on the *Jolly Roger,* about to walk the plank. Sounds of danger surround you, but one is more frightening than the others. What is it? To find out, read the story that begins on the next page. Answer the questions in the margin while you read.

PETER PAN

by J. M. Barrie

What is going to happen?

What is Wendy to do now?

No words of mine can tell you how Wendy despised those pirates. To the boys there was at least some glamour in the pirate calling; but all that she saw was that the ship had not been scrubbed for years. There was not a port-hole on the grimy glass of which you might not have written with your finger "Dirty pig"; and she had already written it on several. But as the boys gathered round her she had no thought, of course, save for them.

"So, my beauty," said Hook, as if he spoke in syrup, "you are to see your children walk the plank."

Fine gentleman though he was, the intensity of his communings had soiled his ruff, and suddenly he knew that she was gazing at it. With a hasty gesture he tried to hide it, but he was too late.

"Are they to die?" asked Wendy, with a look of such frightful contempt that he nearly fainted.

"They are," he snarled. "Silence all," he called gloatingly, "for a mother's last words to her children."

At this moment Wendy was grand. "These are my last words, dear boys," she said firmly. "I feel that I have a message to you from your real mothers, and it is this: 'We hope our sons will die like English gentlemen.'"

Even the pirates were awed; and Tootles cried out hysterically, "I am going to do what my mother hopes. What are you to do, Nibs?"

"What my mother hopes. What are you to do, Twin?"

"What my mother hopes. John, what are—"

But Hook had found his voice again.

"Tie her up," he shouted.

It was Smee who tied her to the mast. "See here, honey," he whispered, "I'll save you if you promise to be my mother."

But not even for Smee would she make such a promise. "I would almost rather have no children at all," she said disdainfully.

It is sad to know that not a boy was looking at her as Smee tied her to the mast; the eyes of all were on the plank: that last little walk they were about to take. They were no longer able to hope that they would walk it manfully, for the capacity to think had gone from them; they could stare and shiver only.

Hook smiled on them with his teeth closed, and took a step toward Wendy. His intention was to turn her face so that she should see the boys walking the plank one by one. But he never reached her, he never heard the cry of anguish he hoped to wring from her. He heard something else instead.

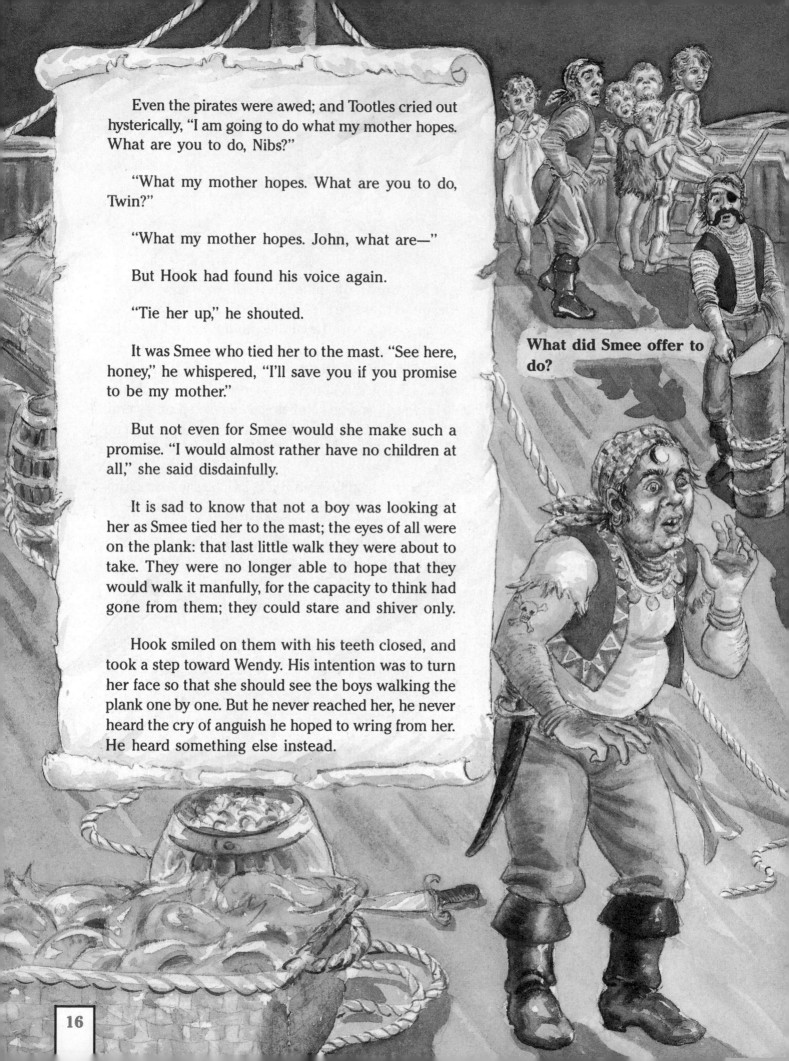

What did Smee offer to do?

What did Hook hear?

What thought was on everyone's mind?

It was the terrible tick-tick of the crocodile.

They all heard it—pirates, boys, Wendy; and immediately every head was blown in one direction; not to the water whence the sound proceeded, but toward Hook. All knew that what was about to happen concerned him alone, and that from being actors they were suddenly become spectators.

Very frightful was it to see the change that came over him. It was as if he had been clipped at every joint. He fell in a little heap.

The sound came steadily nearer; and in advance of it came this ghastly thought, "The crocodile is about to board the ship."

17

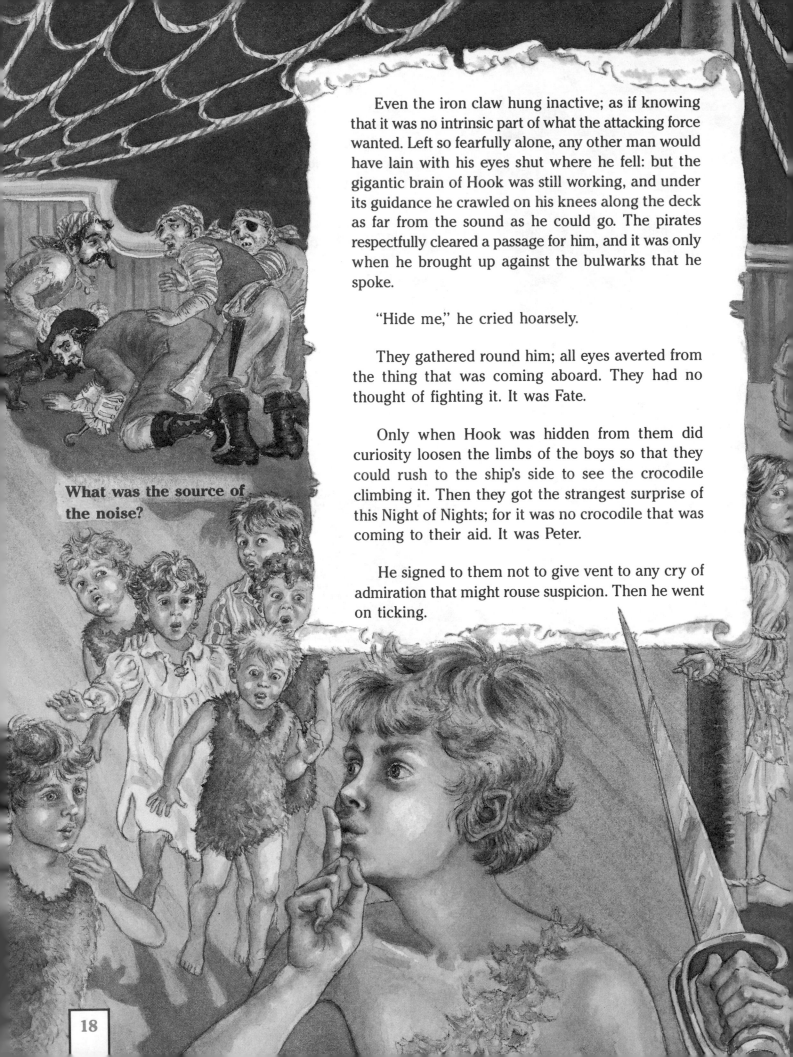

Even the iron claw hung inactive; as if knowing that it was no intrinsic part of what the attacking force wanted. Left so fearfully alone, any other man would have lain with his eyes shut where he fell: but the gigantic brain of Hook was still working, and under its guidance he crawled on his knees along the deck as far from the sound as he could go. The pirates respectfully cleared a passage for him, and it was only when he brought up against the bulwarks that he spoke.

"Hide me," he cried hoarsely.

They gathered round him; all eyes averted from the thing that was coming aboard. They had no thought of fighting it. It was Fate.

Only when Hook was hidden from them did curiosity loosen the limbs of the boys so that they could rush to the ship's side to see the crocodile climbing it. Then they got the strangest surprise of this Night of Nights; for it was no crocodile that was coming to their aid. It was Peter.

He signed to them not to give vent to any cry of admiration that might rouse suspicion. Then he went on ticking.

What was the source of the noise?

18

Thinking About What You Read

What did you find out?

1. This story focuses on one sound: the tick-tick of the crocodile. But what other sounds might have been heard on the pirate ship on this Night of Nights? Add four sounds to the list I've started for you.

☆ *the creaking of the old wooden ship* _____

☆ _____

☆ _____

☆ _____

☆ _____

2. We are told that Wendy despised the pirates. The boys, though, found "at least some glamour in the pirate calling." What glamour might there be in being a pirate?

_____

_____

_____

3. In the story there were many different ways of responding to fear. What were those different responses? Who responded in each way? I've written two answers to get you started. Reread the story to find four more.

Tootles cried out hysterically.

Smee tried to bribe Wendy.

_____

_____

_____

_____

4. How was Captain Hook's behavior at the end of the story different from the way he behaved at the beginning? What does that tell you about his character?

_____

_____

_____

How did the author help you read the story?

Before beginning to write a piece of fiction, an author must choose a **point of view** from which to tell the story. A point of view determines what the reader sees through the eyes of the storyteller, or **narrator.**

There are two frequently used points of view: **first-person** and **omniscient,** or all-knowing. Let's look at these points of view separately.

In a story that has a first-person point of view, the narrator is one of the characters. This character can describe his or her own thoughts and actions, as well as what he or she sees happening to the other characters. But the narrator cannot describe what is in the minds of other characters in the story. The first story you read in this book, *Mischling, Second Degree,* had a first-person point of view.

In a story with an omniscient point of view, though, the narrator might not even be an actual character in the story. Therefore, he or she can describe what is in all the characters' minds, as well as everything that happens to them.

Happily for us, Mr. Barrie chose to use an omniscient point of view in his story. So we learn what all the characters are doing, seeing, hearing, thinking, and feeling. And we get to know the characters very well indeed.

Let's look at how the omniscient point of view helps us to enjoy Mr. Barrie's story.

1. Reread the first paragraph of the story. What two things do we learn about Wendy's thoughts in this paragraph?

   _____

   _____

2. What one thing do we learn about the boys' thoughts in this same paragraph?

   _____

   _____

3. Now look at the third paragraph of the story. What does the narrator tell us Hook knew?

   _____

4. Now turn to page 17. Circle one sentence on the page that tells what everyone knew and one sentence that tells what everyone thought.

5. Think of other stories you've read. Which do you like better—stories with a first-person or an omniscient point of view? Why?

   _____

   _____

   _____

How can you use the omniscient point of view to give readers more details about your characters?

Pretend that Peter unfortunately did not arrive to rescue the children aboard the *Jolly Roger*. The boys are about to walk the plank; Wendy is being forced to watch. What happens next? How will they be rescued? Continue the story about the boys and Wendy. Use some of the words spoken by the characters in the story you read. Also, be sure to write your story in the omniscient point of view. Tell your readers the thoughts and feelings of *all* the characters.

_____

_____

_____

_____

_____

_____

_____

_____

_____

_____

_____

_____

_____

_____

_____

_____

_____

_____

_____

_____

_____

_____

Getting Ready to Read

1. What do these posters show? What might be their purpose?

_____

_____

_____

2. You already know some facts about the Civil War. List three of them below.

☆ _____

☆ _____

☆ _____

3. If you had been a soldier in the Civil War, what sounds of danger might you have heard? What would have made the sounds? Add three ideas to the list I've started for you.

☆ _*another soldier yelling, "Here they come!"*_____

☆ _____

☆ _____

☆ _____

Reading

Now read the poem that begins on the next page. As you read, think of other sounds of danger you might add to your list. Answer the questions in the margin while you read.

Thunder at Gettysburg

by
Patricia Lee
Gauch

What will Tillie see?

BAROOM
"Pa! Ma!
Come quick. It's starting,"
Tillie yelled
as she pulled up her skirts
and took the stairs two by two.
She wasn't going to miss this.
Bobby Schultz had already
climbed into his loft to watch.
The Jenning girls were on their porch roof.
Flocks of folk were watching
and waving
right from High Street.
But Tillie knew where she was heading.
Her own attic.
Quickly she grabbed a chair
and pulled it up to the skylight.
She looked away over the alleys
and roofs and gardens
of Gettysburg.
She could see so clearly,
and sure enough, there they were.

Swarms of blue soldiers—her soldiers—
and swarms of gray
melting toward Seminary Ridge,
just west of town.
And horsemen in rows.
And there, spinning out behind them,
wagon after wagon after wagon.
"Close your mouth, Till,"
her father said from the doorway.
"You'll catch a fly!"
But Tillie couldn't help it.
A week ago she had wished
for Union troops to fight the Rebels.
Wished hard.
Now here they were, finally fighting them.
Her ma and pa talked a lot
about this war.
They said black men and women
and children wouldn't be slaves
ever again
if the Union won.
They said America wouldn't be split
in two if the Union won.
But Tillie didn't know
so much about that.
All she knew for sure was
Snap Rouzer and Davey Robinson
and a whole lot of other Gettysburg boys
went off to fight this war.

What would happen if the Union won the war?

24

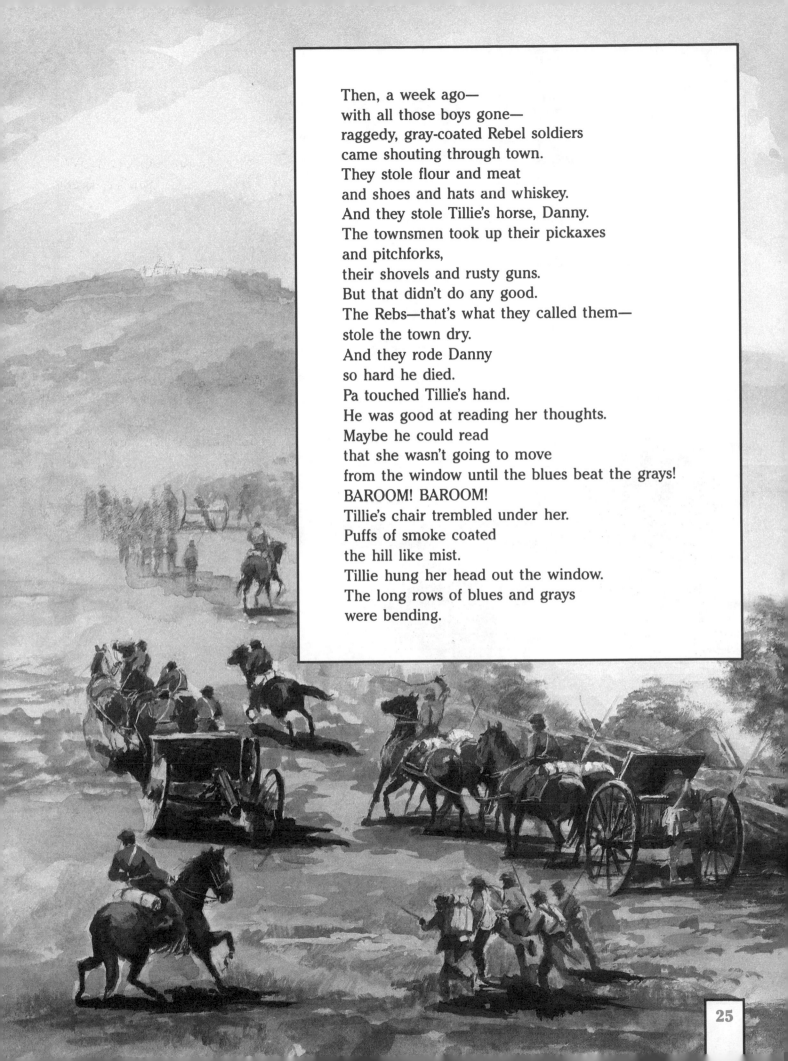

Then, a week ago—
with all those boys gone—
raggedy, gray-coated Rebel soldiers
came shouting through town.
They stole flour and meat
and shoes and hats and whiskey.
And they stole Tillie's horse, Danny.
The townsmen took up their pickaxes
and pitchforks,
their shovels and rusty guns.
But that didn't do any good.
The Rebs—that's what they called them—
stole the town dry.
And they rode Danny
so hard he died.
Pa touched Tillie's hand.
He was good at reading her thoughts.
Maybe he could read
that she wasn't going to move
from the window until the blues beat the grays!
BAROOM! BAROOM!
Tillie's chair trembled under her.
Puffs of smoke coated
the hill like mist.
Tillie hung her head out the window.
The long rows of blues and grays
were bending.

CAK! CAK!
They were shooting!
"Good!" Tillie whispered.
Her father seemed awfully quiet.
Tillie couldn't read his thoughts
so well,
but she was excited.
What a great place to watch a war!
Now the lines seemed to be breaking.
Grays rushing down the hill,
blues climbing up,
horses running wild,
and cannons like thunder rumbling
over and over.
It seemed like such thundering
had to come to something—
any moment—right before her eyes.
Tillie stretched higher,
when suddenly a voice called out.

What happened?

26

Thinking About What You Read

What did you find out?

1. Look back at the sounds of danger you wrote on page 22. What other sounds could you add to your list, now that you've read the poem?

_____   _____

_____   _____

2. Was watching the battle from rooftops, attics, and streets a wise thing to do? Why or why not?

_____

_____

3. Did the Rebs have any right to the flour, meat, shoes, and other goods they took from the people of Gettysburg? What makes you think that?

_____

_____

4. What two reasons for the war were given in the poem? Which do you think was the most important? In your own words, write the reasons in order of their importance.

☆ _____

_____

☆ _____

_____

5. Tillie was excited by the battle. Do you think she SHOULD have been excited? Why do you think so?

_____

_____

How did the poet help you read the poem?

"Thunder at Gettysburg" is a **narrative poem,** or a story told in verse form. (No, this poem doesn't rhyme. But writing doesn't have to rhyme to be poetry, does it?) The purpose of a narrative poem is to tell the story of an event, a person, or an experience. Narrative poems are often used to describe unforgettable or extraordinary events or people.

Ms. Gauch certainly could have told Tillie's story without using this form of poetry. I think, though, that poetry helped make the story more vivid for us. Let's look at why that is.

1. Turn to the beginning of the poem and let your eyes just float quickly down the lines. What happened? Did some lines stand out more than others? Go back and put a check beside those lines.

2. Now look more closely at the lines you checked. How are they alike?

_____

_____

3. What information do the lines you checked give you? How important are these lines to your understanding and enjoyment of the poem?

_____

_____

As you can see, the narrative poem form helped Ms. Gauch make key words and ideas stand out for us. By varying the length of her lines, she could present important thoughts or key words forcefully and dramatically in a short line and then explain them in a longer one. This makes our reading of the poem more exciting and enjoyable.

How can you use the narrative poem form to tell a story?

Choose an important event or person you are studying now in social studies or science as the subject for a narrative poem. Then complete the form below about your choice.

My subject: _____

Characters:

_____   _____

_____   _____

Setting (place and time): _____

Plot summary (what will happen in my poem): _____

_____

_____

_____

_____

Now imagine YOU ARE THERE and write a narrative poem to tell your story. Use short lines to emphasize key words or important ideas and long lines for explanation. Give your poem a title.

_____

4

Getting Ready to Read

Just last spring a robin built a nest in a fern that hangs under our porch roof. The nest of twigs, grasses, and string soon held four light blue eggs. About three weeks later the nest held four newly hatched babies!

1. Imagine what it must be like to be in this nest. What would you—a baby bird—see, hear, and feel? Add some of your own ideas to the chart below.

See	Hear	Feel
branches	*rustling leaves*	*cool breezes*
Mom	chirping	wind

2. What dangers would you, as a nestling, face? What warnings of danger would you have? How might you react to those warnings to protect yourself and the other nestlings? Again, add your ideas to the chart.

Danger	Warning	Reaction
owl coming	*shadow*	*be still*
owl	hoot	be still

3. The information in these charts relates directly to the next story. What are two questions you would like to have answered as you read?

☆ _____

☆ _____

Reading

Keep an eye out for the answers to your own questions as you read *The Cry of the Crow.* Answer the questions in the margin while you read.

The Cry of the Crow

by
Jean
Craighead
George

What did the nestling hear?

Now what did she hear?

The young crow huddled against her brother in their stick nest in Piney Woods. Her tail feathers were short and stubby; white plumes of down trimmed her head. Her milky-blue eyes were those of an eyas, a nestling bird yet unable to stand on her toes or fly. The pair sat rock still, for their parents were away.

The March dawn was hot and muggy. Insects buzzed around the nest, their glassy wings reflecting the red sunlight. The little female looked past them to a spider spinning her web almost a quarter of a mile away. Her eyes were like telescopes, and she practiced using them while she sat in the nest. Her brother slept, a black lump blending with the black sticks.

Footsteps sounded on the pine needles below and the eyas listened to their beat. *Crunch da dum.* She tensed, for she recognized the footfall of the crow hunter. Her parents had taught her a deep fear of this sound. "Ca! Ca! Ca! Ca!" they would cry at the sound, then pull their feathers against their bodies and crouch silently.

The footfall softened and died away.

What was the next sound she heard?

What did the eyas listen for?

Wide-awake now, the eyas heard her parents announce from the Glades that they were on their way home with food. Her ears were as keen as her eyesight. She could distinguish the sounds of her parents' voices from all the other crows of Piney Woods as well as from the clan of crows in Trumpet Hammock, a tree island in the saw grass of the Everglades, a swamplike river that creeps slowly down the tip of Florida under warm subtropical skies.

As her parents flew home, the eyas listened for the voice of the Piney Woods guard crow. He had not warned of the *crunch da dum,* nor did he announce her parents. The forest was ominously quiet and had been ever since the crow hunters began shooting a few days ago.

With a rustle of feathers, her mother alighted on the edge of the nest.

"Ah ah ah cowkle, cowkle," the eyas begged as she lay on her breast, trembling her wings and opening her beak. Her bill was rimmed with yellow edges. She could not yet eat by herself, for she was only ten days old, and since food had to be thrust in her mouth, the red-and-yellow coloring made it possible for her parents to find the gullet instantly. Her mother stuffed her with delicacies from the Everglades.

What happened?

Her father arrived, his feathers glistening blue-black in the soft morning light. Her brother begged for food.

From below came a gun blast. Lead balls ripped through the stick nest. Her father jerked backward, his eyes exploding. Her mother spun around in a burst of feathers. Another blast ripped through her brother and lifted the nest out of the tree crotch. The young eyas gripped a stick as the nest splintered, cracked, then floated apart. She looked down through the pieces and saw the eye and brow of the hunter.

"I got youv," he shouted. The voice and eye were stamped forever on the young crow's mind.

Then she fell.

Thinking About What You Read

What did you find out?

1. There were many sounds mentioned in this story. Some of them were *not* dangerous. These were normal everyday sounds that the eyas had learned to recognize. Other sounds, however—or missing sounds—were signals of danger. Complete the lists below. Classify all of the sounds mentioned or suggested in the story into everyday sounds or signals of danger.

Everyday Sounds	Signals of Danger
_____	_____
_____	_____
_____	_____
_____	_____
_____	_____

2. Why do you think the guard crow failed to announce the danger?

_____

_____

_____

3. When the footfall softened and died away, what was the hunter doing? How do you know that?

_____

_____

_____

4. The last sentence of the story is "Then she fell." Do you think the eyas died? Why or why not?

_____

_____

_____

How did the author help you read the story?

You can tell that Jean Craighead George knows a lot about crows and their habitats, the places where they live. She realized, though, that we might not know as much about these things as she does. So in order for us to understand what she was saying, she defined some terms for us. And she did this very cleverly. She gave us the term, and then she immediately told us what it was. Let's see if you can find some examples of Ms. George's definitions.

1. Reread the story and find the sentences in which the terms *eyas, Trumpet Hammock,* and *Everglades* are used for the first time. Underline those sentences.

2. Go back and read those sentences again. Circle the new term and its definition.

3. Now look once more at each sentence. What punctuation mark follows each new term? Write the name of that mark on the feather at the right.

Ms. George helped us to understand new terms and information with **context clues,** or definitions given in the same or following sentence. Ha! You see, I just did it. I gave you a context clue for *context clues.* Authors often use context clues so that readers can read a whole story without having to run to the dictionary to look up new words. It's really an excellent—quick and easy—way to make your vocabulary grow!

4. Just one more thing before we go on.... Look at the first paragraph on this page. In the first sentence, what word did I give you a context clue for? Write one letter of the word on each tree.

How can you use context clues to help readers understand new words?

Ms. George's story is told by an observer of the action. Think about the story and see it through the eyes of a DIFFERENT observer: a rabbit hidden in nearby bushes, another crow passing overhead, or a hiker watching from behind a tree. How would each of these observers report the events of the story? On the next page are the three new observers. Write their reports of the action in their speech balloons. Be sure to use at least one context clue in each report.

_____
_____
_____
_____
_____
_____
_____
_____
_____

_____
_____
_____
_____
_____
_____
_____
_____

_____
_____
_____
_____
_____
_____
_____
_____
_____
_____

Getting Ready to Read

1. Once, long ago, there were no people on the earth. In fact, the planet itself was young and just taking shape. How did the earth's features—mountains, oceans, islands, continents—come to be the way we know them today? On the lines below, write a few facts about the formation of the earth's surface.

_____

_____

_____

_____

2. Today our knowledge of how the earth's surface formed comes from scientific studies. Scientists use computers to make models of how the earth used to be and how it has changed over time. Long ago, though, people had their own ideas about how the world took shape. Those people made up stories to explain the things they didn't understand. Do you know an old tale that explains how something came to be, or why an object is the way it is? Write it on the lines below.

_____

_____

_____

_____

_____

Reading

The tale that begins on the next page is a very old one. It tries to explain how one part of the world—where China and Taiwan are—came to look as it does today. Read the folktale to find out just how imaginative people were long ago. Answer the questions in the margin while you read.

How the Dragon Lost His Tail

by Cora Cheney

Once long ago before the Jade Emperor put people on the earth, China was a great sleeping father dragon lying in the shape of a perfect circle with only the tip of his tail sticking out into the sea.

In the China Sea the young dragons played about, splashing the water into little storms, breathing wispy clouds, and fighting each other to make tiny typhoons for the annoyance of the world.

The young dragons finally tired of this sport.

"I want Father to wake up and make us a great storm," said the first little dragon.

"I want Father to wake up and breathe fearful black clouds," said the second little dragon.

"I want Father to wake up and make a fierce typhoon," said the third little dragon.

What was the dragon?

What did the little dragons decide to do?

What sound did the little dragons hear?

But the father dragon continued to sleep. The little dragons became more restless.

"Let's wake our father. He has been sleeping too long," said the little dragons.

So the first little dragon made a rush through the sea and nipped at the big dragon who was still coiled in a circle. He made a small dent in the circle.

Then the second little dragon took a bite, and the third little dragon followed the example. The father dragon stirred but he did not awaken.

Nip, nip—the young dragons grew bolder, taking out great bits and pieces of their father's scaly back, eating into the perfect circle, spitting bites into the water.

Finally the father dragon woke up with a roar that made the earth tremble. He lashed his tail so hard that the tip, weakened by so many bites, broke off and fell into the sea with a crashing splash. A little dragon was trapped underneath.

The father dragon was so angry that he turned over to the south of China and stretched out with his head to the west and his cut-off tail to the east and went back to sleep.

Today, what is the father dragon's tail tip?

What is the father dragon called now?

On the map today you can see the lashed-off tail tip. It is the Island of Taiwan. The mountain range down the middle of the island is the little dragon underneath. The ragged seacoast of China shows where the bites came out, and to the south of China lies the forbidding father dragon himself, sleeping away his anger. They call him the Himalaya Mountains on the map.

But not shown on the map are the naughty young dragons who play about in the Taiwan Straits and the China Sea causing typhoons, storms, or just wispy clouds.

Thinking About What You Read

What did you find out?

1. How did the three young dragons feel when they tired of their little games? How did the father dragon feel when he was so rudely awakened? Add three more descriptive words to each of the lists I've started for you.

Young Dragons	Father Dragon
bored	*annoyed*

2. How do you think the father dragon would feel if he knew that his tail had trapped one of the little dragons? Why?

_____

3. In what order did the events listed below occur in the story? Number the events *1* to *4* to show the order in which they happened.

_____ The Himalaya Mountains were formed in the south of China.

_____ The mountain range on Taiwan was formed.

_____ The seacoast of China was formed.

_____ The Island of Taiwan broke off from the mainland.

4. Look at the map on page 40. Why do you think the people who made up this tale thought southern China and Taiwan looked like a sleeping dragon and the tip of a dragon's tail? Do you agree with them? Why or why not?

_____

_____

_____

5. Why is this story included in a unit called SOUNDS OF DANGER?

_____

_____

41

Isn't this a delightful folktale? Even though Ms. Cheney's version is very short, she still painted some wonderful pictures for us.

One way authors paint pictures for their readers is with **figurative language.** Figurative language is descriptive language that makes comparisons. It describes one thing by saying that it is like something else. **Similes** and **metaphors** are two kinds of figurative language. Let's take a closer look at these ways of describing things.

A simile uses *like* or *as* to compare two very different things. Each of these sentences, for example, contains a simile:

> *The China Sea was **like glass.***
> *The little dragon was **as annoying as a toothache.***

Now, you know that a sea and glass aren't similar things, and a dragon and a toothache aren't alike either. But using similes to compare these very different things certainly creates some great images, doesn't it?

A metaphor, on the other hand, suggests a likeness between two things by saying that one thing IS the other. Metaphors do NOT contain *like* or *as*. For example, this sentence contains a metaphor:

> *The storm cloud was **a locomotive roaring across the sky.***

Of course, a storm cloud isn't really a locomotive. But this comparison gives us a powerful picture of what the cloud looked like.

1. Ms. Cheney's entire story is based on a metaphor stated right at the beginning. What is it?

_____

_____

2. There are three more metaphors in the story, too. Can you find them? Finish these sentences by writing the correct metaphors.

Today, the father dragon's tail tip is _____

_____.

The mountain range down the middle of Taiwan is _____

_____.

On the map, the sleeping father dragon is now _____

_____.

3. Now try to write your own simile and metaphor. Write two sentences about dragons. Use a simile in one and a metaphor in the other.

☆ _____

_____

☆ _____

_____

How can similes and metaphors help you paint vivid pictures for your readers?

On a physical map of the world, find where you live. Then make up a tale to explain how your area came to look as it does today. How did it get its shape? How were its geographical features formed? Use at least two similes and two metaphors in your tale to give your readers a clear and vivid picture of how your area took shape.

_____

_____

_____

_____

_____

_____

_____

_____

_____

_____

_____

_____

_____

_____

_____

UNIT TWO

A MATTER OF TIME

1. How are all of the things pictured above alike?

_____

_____

Time is a very important feature of our lives. We plan and live our days according to schedules. In fact, we often even plan our years, so that we can make the most of our time.

2. Each word below has some connection to time. What time-related object could you use to represent each word? Draw your object in the space under each word. Then choose a color that the word suggests to you. Circle the word and your drawing with that color.

growth   silence   explosion

suspense   endurance   imagination

As you might guess, each story in this unit concerns A MATTER OF TIME. But just _how_ will time feature in each story? Well, let's go find out!

Getting Ready to Read

1. If you wanted to hire an airplane pilot, how would you word your advertisement? Write the copy for your ad here.

_____

_____

2. Good news! Several people have answered your ad. Now you have to interview them. What are two questions you'll be sure to ask?

☆ _____

☆ _____

3. Suppose the year is 1928. The person you think you want to hire would be the first woman to fly across the Atlantic Ocean. What two additional questions would you want to ask her?

☆ _____

☆ _____

4. You've probably figured out that the next story is about Amelia Earhart. At the time of this flight, Amelia didn't have the experience to pilot the plane, but she did serve as captain. Her crew members were Bill Stultz, the pilot, and Slim Gordon, the mechanic. As captain, Amelia had to make all final decisions connected with the flight. What are two decisions she may have been called on to make during this historic flight?

☆ _____

☆ _____

Reading

Now read the story that begins on the next page to find out what decisions Amelia actually made. Answer the questions in the margin while you read.

LOST STAR
The Story of Amelia Earhart

by Patricia Lauber

Where did the fliers begin their flight?

In late May they were ready. Two attempts to get away from Boston failed because the weather was against them. When they finally were able to take off, they headed straight up the coast and ran into thick fog. Since there were no instruments for flying blind at that time, they looked for a hole in the fog and landed at Halifax, Nova Scotia.

The next day was beautifully clear, with just the right wind. They flew to Trepassey, Newfoundland, their starting point for the Atlantic flight, and landed to take on fuel. But weather and mechanical difficulties trapped them for thirteen long days. Strong winds churned the bay, making takeoff impossible. A pontoon sprung a leak and an oil tank cracked. Slim repaired them. The fliers passed their time playing rummy, chopping wood, studying maps and weather reports, hiking, and fishing. Under strain, Bill began drinking heavily, but Slim thought he would be all right once they were in the air.

On June 12 they tried for the second time to take off. The plane felt heavy. They got rid of cameras, coats, bags, everything they could spare. They still could not take off. The next day they unloaded 200 gallons of fuel. This lessened both their margin of safety and their cruising range. With only 700 gallons of gasoline they could at best reach Ireland. But even with the lighter load they still could not get off.

Amelia had a decision to make. There was a backup pilot waiting in Boston in case he was needed. Should she send for him? She was tempted to. But if she did, she would hurt Bill and greatly harm his career. She might even endanger the whole project. In the end, she decided to stay with Bill and hope that the weather would take a turn for the better before he cracked up.

What decision did Amelia have to make?

Finally, in late morning of June 17, 1928, the wind was in the right direction, and the weather forecast seemed promising. Amelia and Slim got Bill out of bed and helped him aboard the plane.

Three times Bill taxied into position, facing the wind. Three times the plane charged down the bay but could not get up enough speed to take off. They tried a fourth time. As before, Amelia was crouched in the cabin with a stop watch in hand to check the take-off time. Her eyes were fixed on the speed indicator. They would have to reach a speed of at least fifty-five miles an hour for *Friendship* to take off. Thirty . . . forty . . . fifty . . . fifty-five . . . sixty—they were off at last.

What happened?

With two engines sputtering from salt spray, they climbed to 3,000 feet and ran into fog. They climbed higher and met a snowstorm. Bill headed down and they broke into clear skies and sunshine, with a blue sea below them. It didn't last. They were soon either flying through clouds or above them. Amelia was entranced by what she was seeing—the shapes of the clouds, the pink tint added by the setting sun, the gray hollows and shadows. She later wrote that she had spent her time kneeling at the window "gulping beauty."

In the north, summer nights are short, and they were flying east, toward the sun. They flew through only five hours of darkness. But even in daylight fog kept them from seeing the ocean, and their radio had stopped working. They could not get word from ships at sea to check their position.

About the time they thought they should be reaching Ireland, Bill dropped down through the clouds and fog. They were hoping to see land, because their gas was getting low. There was no land in sight, but they did see a big transatlantic ship. If it had left Ireland and they were headed for Ireland, plane and ship should have been on parallel courses. They weren't. The ship was cutting directly across their course. Did this mean they were lost? It was an unpleasant thought.

What new problem arose?

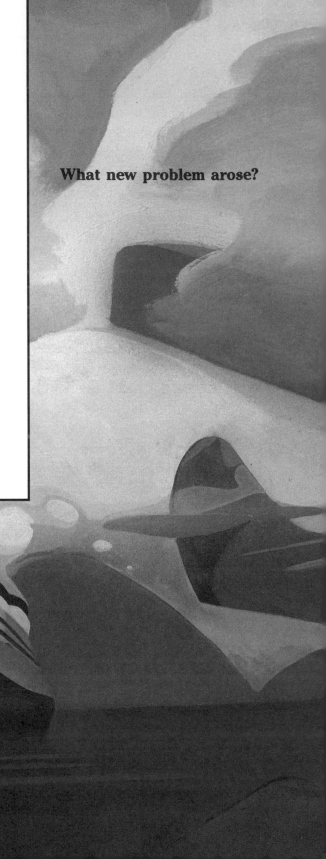

What did they need to know?

What new decision had to be made?

They circled the ship, hoping the captain would guess what they wanted and have the ship's position painted on the deck so that they could read it. When nothing happened, Amelia wrote their request on a piece of paper, put it in a bag weighted with two oranges, and dropped it through the hatch in the cabin floor. The message fell into the sea.

To go on circling was to waste fuel. Their choices were to ditch near the ship and be picked up or to go on. They chose to go on. It was the right decision. Soon they saw two small fishing boats, a sign that land was near, then another transatlantic ship. As it turned out, they had passed Ireland and were now approaching Wales. They saw a little town and decided to land there. Bill set the *Friendship* down in the harbor and taxied to a buoy, where they tied up.

Thanks to the skill of Bill Stultz, they had arrived safely, after a flight of twenty hours, forty minutes, and for the first time a woman had crossed the Atlantic by air. But because the plane's radio was not working, there was no way they could send out word of their achievement.

Thinking About What You Read

What did you find out?

1. Of the decisions Amelia made between June 12 and June 16, which was the most difficult? Why was it so difficult?

_____

_____

_____

2. Near the end of their flight, the crew members were not sure where they were. They decided to go on, at the risk of running out of fuel, rather than ditch the plane near the ship they saw. Is this the decision you would have made? Why or why not?

_____

_____

_____

3. What else do you think Amelia could have done to try to signal the ship below?

_____

_____

4. The crew thought they only had enough fuel to reach Ireland, but they landed in Wales, which is east of Ireland. How do you think they could have made that mistake in their calculations?

_____

_____

_____

5. After Amelia and her crew landed, she was suddenly the most famous aviatrix in the world. Everyone wanted to see her and interview her. But Amelia felt she had been only a passenger on the flight, so she felt guilty about her fame. Do you think she was right to feel this way? Why?

_____

_____

_____

How did the author help you read the story?

Everybody makes decisions. Some are easy to make; others are hard. Some decisions offer many choices; others offer few. All decisions have two things in common: a reason for having to make it and a result. The reason for making a decision is its **cause**. The result of making the decision is its **effect**.

In this story, Ms. Lauber used causes and effects to help us understand exactly what happened on the *Friendship*'s history-making flight. Let's look a little more closely at the cause/effect relationships we saw in the story.

1. Reread the story to complete this chart of causes and effects. I've written one to get you started.

Causes		Effects
bad weather in Boston	→	*couldn't take off*
no instruments for flying blind	→	_____
limited fuel	→	_____
_____	→	make repairs and pass time
continued delay in Newfoundland	→	_____
_____	→	discard everything possible
possibility of hurting Bill and damaging his career	→	_____

2. Finally, the weather was clear (cause), and the plane took off (effect). Now list as many other cause/effect relationships as you can think of that occurred during the flight.

Cause	Effect
☆ _____	☆ _____
☆ _____	☆ _____
☆ _____	☆ _____
☆ _____	☆ _____
☆ _____	☆ _____
☆ _____	☆ _____

How can you use cause/effect statements to present information clearly?

Imagine that you are a radio reporter. You are about to interview one of the crew of the *Friendship*. What questions would you include in your interview? What answers would you get? Write a short script of this interview on the lines below. Be sure to use cause/effect statements to make the questions and answers clear. When your script is finished, ask a friend to take the part of the crew member. Read your interview to your class.

Getting Ready to Read

Lion tamers, movie stuntpeople, race car drivers, and paratroopers are some people who gladly walk (run, jump, or fly) into the face of danger. These people actually LIKE taking risks! But how do YOU feel about taking risks?

1. Take the test below to find your Risk-Taking Score. First, decide how willing you'd be to take each risk listed on the left. Then circle a number on the scale to show your degree of eagerness to take each risk. The numbers range from *1* (would never do it) to *5* (would eagerly do it).

RISK-TAKING TEST

A. Go away on a UFO with some strange beings   1   2   3   4   5

B. Find yourself in a cave with a bear that's just waking after a winter's sleep   1   2   3   4   5

C. Wander off a mountain trail with night coming on   1   2   3   4   5

D. Walk through a cemetery at night alone   1   2   3   4   5

E. Substitute for the lion tamer—before the lion's had breakfast   1   2   3   4   5

F. Enter a big, dark closet in a huge room in a strange, creaky old house   1   2   3   4   5

G. Follow Alice down the rabbit hole   1   2   3   4   5

H. Go white-water rafting in an old rowboat— without a guide   1   2   3   4   5

I. Walk alone into a tall, dark, dense forest   1   2   3   4   5

J. Use your uncle's power tools without asking   1   2   3   4   5

Now add up all the circled numbers.
Write your total Risk-Taking Score
on the line. _____

Well, how did you measure up? Use this chart to interpret your results.

If Your Score Is:	Consider Yourself:
5 – 15	A Cream Puff
16 – 35	A Brave Adventurer
36 – 50	A Reckless Daredevil

2. Look back at risk *F* on the chart. Under what circumstances would you take this risk? Write your answer on the side of the big, old, strange, creaky house.

Now think for a few seconds about how boring a rainy, dreary day can be. Don't you long for something interesting to do? Even with other people around, rainy days can be DULL!

But suppose you found yourself in a strange house one rainy day, looking for something—anything—to do. Would you be ready to take a risk? Hmmm?

3. Look at the title of the story that begins on the next page. What is one question you expect the story to answer for you?

_____

_____

_____

Reading

Now read the story to find out if it answers your question. Answer the questions in the margin while you read.

The Lion, the Witch and the Wardrobe

by C. S. Lewis

Who stayed behind and why?

"Nothing there!" said Peter, and they all trooped out again—all except Lucy. She stayed behind because she thought it would be worth while trying the door of the wardrobe, even though she felt almost sure that it would be locked. To her surprise it opened quite easily, and two moth-balls dropped out.

Looking into the inside, she saw several coats hanging up—mostly long fur coats. There was nothing Lucy liked so much as the smell and feel of fur. She immediately stepped into the wardrobe and got in among the coats and rubbed her face against them, leaving the door open, of course, because she knew that it is very foolish to shut oneself into any wardrobe. Soon she went further in and found that there was a second row of coats hanging up behind the first one. It was almost quite dark in there and she kept her arms stretched out in front of her so as not to bump her face into the back of the wardrobe. She took a step further in—then two or three steps—always expecting to feel woodwork against the tips of her fingers. But she could not feel it.

"This must be a simply enormous wardrobe!" thought Lucy, going still further in and pushing the soft folds of the coats aside to make room for her. Then she noticed that there was something crunching under her feet. "I wonder is that more moth-balls?" she thought, stooping down to feel it with her hands. But instead of feeling the hard, smooth wood of the floor of the wardrobe, she felt something soft and powdery and extremely cold. "This is very queer," she said, and went on a step or two further.

Next moment she found that what was rubbing against her face and hands was no longer soft fur but something hard and rough and even prickly. "Why, it is just like branches of trees!" exclaimed Lucy. And then she saw that there was a light ahead of her; not a few inches away where the back of the wardrobe ought to have been, but a long way off. Something cold and soft was falling on her. A moment later she found that she was standing in the middle of a wood at night-time with snow under her feet and snowflakes falling through the air.

What did Lucy touch?

Where was Lucy standing?

56

Lucy felt a little frightened, but she felt very inquisitive and excited as well. She looked back over her shoulder and there, between the dark tree-trunks, she could still see the open doorway of the wardrobe and even catch a glimpse of the empty room from which she had set out. (She had, of course, left the door open, for she knew that it is a very silly thing to shut oneself into a wardrobe.) It seemed to be still daylight there. "I can always get back if anything goes wrong," thought Lucy. She began to walk forward, *crunch-crunch,* over the snow and through the wood towards the other light.

In about ten minutes she reached it and found that it was a lamp-post. As she stood looking at it, wondering why there was a lamp-post in the middle of a wood and wondering what to do next, she heard a pitter patter of feet coming towards her. And soon after that a very strange person stepped out from among the trees into the light of the lamp-post.

What did she find?

What appeared in the light?

Thinking About What You Read

What did you find out?

1. How did Lucy lower the risk of entering the wardrobe?

_____

2. What other risks might there be in entering a wardrobe?

_____

_____

_____

3. Did you notice anything strange or unusual about time in this story? What was it?

_____

_____

4. Had the snow been falling for some time in the forest? How do you know?

_____

_____

5. When Lucy reached the middle of the road, she turned to look over her shoulder at the room she had left. Was the room a distance from her? How do you know?

_____

_____

6. What effect did being able to see the empty room have on Lucy? How do you think it made her feel?

_____

_____

How did the author help you read the story?

When we read this story, we felt as if we were actually walking through the wardrobe with Lucy. We saw what Lucy saw, felt what she touched, and heard what she heard. This is exactly what Mr. Lewis hoped we would do! And because we DID experience these things so vividly, we were able to enjoy the story a great deal.

Wouldn't you like to be able to tell a story the way Mr. Lewis told this one? Of course you would! So let's see if we can discover just how Mr. Lewis gave us the feeling of actually being there with Lucy.

1. Look at the list below on the left. Then reread the story to find all the words Mr. Lewis used to describe how each of these things *felt*. Write the words in the column on the right. I've done the first one to get you started. (HINT: You should find more than one word for each thing!)

Things in the Story	Words That Describe Them
fur	*soft* _____
snow	_____
wood of the floor	_____
branches of trees	_____

2. Now scan the story once again. Find two different places where Mr. Lewis used a two-word term to describe how something *sounded*. Write each term in the snowbank. Then below the snowbank, tell briefly what each term describes.

Have you noticed anything special about how Mr. Lewis wrote his story? Right! He used a lot of **descriptive words.** Descriptive words tell how things look, sound, feel, smell, and taste. They make what we read or write come alive. Mr. Lewis, a master storyteller, used descriptive words in order to make Lucy's trip through the wardrobe real for us.

3. What words do you know that describe how a thing looks, sounds, feels, smells, and tastes? In the columns below, write as many descriptive words as you can. I've written one word in each column to get you started.

Looks	Sounds	Feels	Smells	Tastes
bright	*loud*	*sharp*	*fruity*	*sour*
_____	_____	_____	_____	_____
_____	_____	_____	_____	_____
_____	_____	_____	_____	_____

How can you use descriptive words to make your writing come alive?

Look around your classroom. Is there something in the room that could be the entrance to another world? How would people get into that "other world"? And when they got there, what would they see, hear, feel, smell, and taste?

Describe your "other world" on the lines below. Make your writing come alive by including as many descriptive words as you can. Use the words you listed on page 59 and any others you can think of. When you are done, give your description a title. Then share your writing with a friend. Ask your friend to draw a picture of the world you described. Does your friend's picture match the picture you had in your mind while you were writing?

_____

Getting Ready to Read

Think of it! Time is running out, and the game is on the line. Only one team can win, and these last few minutes—and seconds—will make the difference!

1. Below each picture write a last-minute event that could decide the outcome of the game.

Bottom of the ninth, runner on second, two outs

Fourth quarter, 10 seconds left on the clock

_____

_____

2. Have you ever been in a situation like the ones pictured above? How do you think each of these players feels? Write some words below to describe their feelings.

_____

_____

Reading

This is it—the state championship is on the line! Oh no! The score is tied, the buzzer is waiting to sound, and our team has one free throw! ARGGHHH! Read the poem on page 62 to find out what happens.

FOUL SHOT

by
Edwin A. Hoey

With two 60's stuck on the scoreboard
And two seconds hanging on the clock,
The solemn boy in the center of eyes,
Squeezed by silence,
Seeks out the line with his feet,
Soothes his hands along his uniform,
Gently drums the ball against the floor,
Then measures the waiting net,
Raises the ball on his right hand,
Balances it with his left,
Calms it with fingertips,
Breathes,
Crouches,
Waits,
And then through a stretching of stillness,
Nudges it upward.

The ball slides up and out.
Lands,
Leans,
Wobbles,
Wavers,
Hesitates,
Exasperates,
Plays it coy
Until every face begs with unsounding
                     screams—
And then,
            And then,
                        And then,
Right before ROAR-UP,
Dives down and through.

Thinking About What You Read

What did you find out?

1. I can't look! Did we win? Put the final score up on the scoreboard.

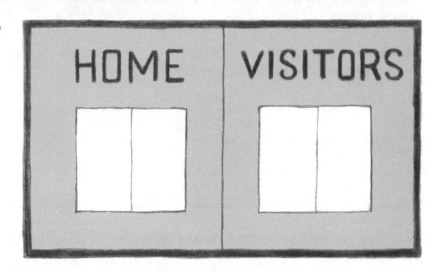

2. How did the boy making the shot feel? How do you know?

_____

_____

_____

3. How did the crowd look? What was going through their minds and showing on their faces? How do you know?

_____

_____

_____

4. What do you think the phrase "Right before ROAR-UP" means? Why do you think so?

_____

_____

_____

How did the poet help you read the poem?

This is one of the most exciting poems I've ever read. And each time I read it, I get excited again. You probably shared my reaction when you read the poem. But just why does it affect us this way? Well, there are at least two reasons. First, Mr. Hoey used very **exact verbs** to describe each detail of the action. Second, he used **single-word lines** to build the suspense and draw out the action. Let's take a closer look at each of these techniques.

First, think about the verbs, or action words, Mr. Hoey used. This poem covers a time period of just two seconds. But as you read, don't you get the feeling that those two seconds have been stretched out somehow? We hold our breaths as we picture every single movement or gesture made by the boy and the ball. It's almost as if we were seeing the boy and the ball in slow motion through a magnifying glass! The reason we get this feeling is because of the amazing number of details Mr. Hoey provided. And the heart of each of those details is the exact verb Mr. Hoey chose.

1. Reread the first stanza. What verbs describe the boy's movements? Find ten more action words to add to the list below.

   seeks

   _____ _____ _____

   _____ _____ _____

   _____ _____ _____

   _____ _____

2. Now reread the second stanza. What verbs describe the ball's flight through the air? Write them below.

   _____ _____ _____

   _____ _____ _____

   _____ _____ _____

Glance quickly through the lists you wrote. Can you see just how much detail those verbs provide? Each time we read them, we get an "instant replay" of the shot in slow motion! The technique of using exact verbs to provide detail helps our suspense grow and grow.

The other way Mr. Hoey built excitement was by using single-word lines.

3. Read through the poem one more time. What happens to your reading speed as you move from the longer lines to the ones that have only one word?

   _____

4. How do these single-word lines, followed by a comma, work to draw us into the action of the poem?

   _____

   _____

   _____

How can you use exact verbs and single-word lines to create exciting poetry?

Athletes really like it when they have support from their fans. One of the ways fans show their support for a team is to cheer! Become a basketball fan (or choose another sport that you like better) and write a cheer for your team. Write your cheer in the form of a poem. Remember to use exact verbs and single-word lines to lead your team to a win!

Getting Ready to Read

What is time? For me, it is the hour and minutes shown on the clock. It's also the countdown of digits on the microwave, or the date of an event I can't wait for. Time for me is also time past: piano recitals, slumber parties, trick-or-treat nights, and the rabbit's funeral in the backyard on a cold, rainy day.

1. What is time for you? Describe your ideas of time here.

_____

_____

_____

_____

2. The words we use to describe time are interesting, too. Do you and your classmates give the same meaning to the various time words we use? Tell what each of the following words in quotation marks means to you.

☆ You say you will wait "forever" for something. How long does that really mean?

_____

_____

☆ You say you'll "never" give up an idea. Just how long is that?

_____

_____

3. Now think about how you USE time. Then tell how you use time in each of the following ways.

☆ waste time _____

☆ save time _____

Reading

The story that begins on page 67 tells how a girl named Sarah used time. Read the story, paying special attention to what Sarah does (and doesn't do). Answer the questions in the margin while you read.

Mama's Going to Buy You a Mockingbird

by Jean Little

What had Jeremy been doing?

"Can I come, too?" Sarah asked.

Jeremy jumped. The dreamy look left his eyes. Lost in his thoughts, he had not known that she was there until she spoke. Now he looked up at her standing on the dock above him.

"No," he said.

"I have my life jacket on."

"No," he repeated, his voice hard.

He gave her no reason for his decision. He knew better. Give Sarah any excuse for an argument and you were asking for trouble. She was like a bulldog; she never gave up. Now, instead of going away, she stayed right where she was and drooped with disappointment. She looked so sad and small that he wanted to hit her.

"You heard me," he told her, stung into speech by her waiting silence. "I said 'No' and I meant it. Do me a favour and scram."

What made Jeremy speak?

Sarah's lips parted, but if she had thought of answering him back, she stopped herself. He had no business ordering her off the dock, and she knew she could get him into trouble with Aunt Margery by telling on him. She also knew that if she tattled, she would never get to go out in the rowboat with him. Well, not today, anyway. She held her tongue and went on waiting.

What did Sarah want to do?

Jeremy turned away. Let her stand there forever. He couldn't care less.

Go ahead and bawl, he thought. See how far it gets you. He pushed back his brown hair which badly needed cutting and studied the cloud formations above the cottage. Then he began to whistle as if he had entirely forgotten her presence.

How did Sarah's behavior make Jeremy feel?

But Sarah Talbot, though she was nearly four years younger than her brother, still knew a few important things about him. One of these was when not to cry. Another was that, tough as he tried to sound, he had a soft heart. She remained visibly hopeful.

Having ignored her for a full minute, Jeremy could not resist darting a glance at her to see how she was taking it. Her head was lowered so that her hair fell forward on either side of her face. She made no sound, not even a whisper of a sigh. Jeremy remembered Dad telling him about a man called Gandhi who had changed the history of India by simply sitting still and waiting for his enemies to give in. At that moment, Jeremy saw why it had worked. Sarah had not begged him or bribed him or threatened him or even tried to explain to him how she was feeling. Yet in some mysterious way, she had put him in the wrong.

Thinking About What You Read

What did you find out?

1. Sarah knew that if she tattled on Jeremy, she'd never get to go out in the rowboat. For Sarah, how long was "never"?

_____

2. Ms. Little wrote that Jeremy ignored Sarah for "a full minute." How could Jeremy know that he had ignored her for a full minute?

_____

_____

3. When have you used time to your advantage, as Sarah did in this story?

_____

_____

_____

_____

_____

4. When has time been used against you, as it was against Jeremy?

_____

_____

_____

_____

_____

5. How did Jeremy feel about his sister? Write one sentence that sums up Jeremy's feelings.

_____

_____

6. What one word would you use to describe Sarah's personality?

_____

How did the author help you read the story?

Jean Little used this first part of her story to introduce us to her characters. In just these few pages, we got a very good idea of the two characters' personalities. What we learned about Sarah and Jeremy was both interesting and clearly presented. Let's think about how Ms. Little gave us so much information in so few words.

The author used three basic *types* of sentences in her story: sentences that simply informed or explained, sentences that told what Sarah said, and sentences that told what Jeremy said. The author also used three basic sentence *lengths:* short, medium, and long. Now let's find out whether there's a **pattern,** or plan, to the way the author used these different types and lengths of sentences.

1. Turn back to the beginning of the story. Reread only the lines of conversation spoken by Sarah and Jeremy. What do you notice about the length of these sentences?

   _____

2. How would the short sentences be spoken? What effect does Jeremy want the short sentences to have?

   _____

   _____

3. How would Sarah's medium-length sentences be spoken? What effect does Sarah want them to have?

   _____

   _____

4. Now look for another place in the story where Ms. Little again uses short sentences to add to your understanding of how Jeremy was feeling about Sarah's request and behavior. Underline these sentences and then look at them again. How are they like the sentences Jeremy spoke?

   _____

   _____

5. Finally, reread the last paragraph of the story. What kind of sentences does Ms. Little use in it? Why?

   _____

   _____

6. Now what can you say about Ms. Little's sentence pattern?

   _____

   _____

How can you use sentences of different lengths to present information in a clear and interesting way?

Let's change Ms. Little's story a little bit. Pretend that Sarah IS the kind of girl who would beg, bribe, or threaten Jeremy, or try to explain her feelings to him. What would happen? How would Jeremy respond? Write a new story below. Include dialogue to show what Sarah and Jeremy say to each other. Use different sentence lengths to make your writing interesting. Share your finished story with some friends. Read it aloud to see how the different sentence lengths sound.

_____

_____

_____

_____

_____

_____

_____

_____

_____

_____

_____

_____

_____

_____

_____

_____

_____

_____

_____

_____

_____

_____

Getting Ready to Read

1. You knew that one, didn't you? I thought so. But wait a minute! Can time really "fly"? Just what does that saying mean?

_____

_____

_____

2. "Time flies" is one saying about time that we use. What other sayings about time do you know? Write some of them here.

☆ _____

☆ _____

☆ _____

Reading

The story that begins on page 74 deals with an old saying about time. Read the story to find out what that saying is. Answer the questions in the margin while you read.

TIME

by Harold Courlander and George Herzog

Once there was a rich man in Africa whose name was Time. He owned more goats, chickens, and cattle than he could count. He possessed more land than he had ever seen, and on his farms were grown vast quantities of rice, manioc, and all kinds of foods. He had immense stores of cloth, and his many granaries were always overflowing with grain. His reputation had spread far beyond his own tribe. Traders came from distant towns to do business with Time. Dancers, acrobats, and wrestlers came to perform for him. Tribes far and wide sent messengers just to see Time face to face and to return and tell the people what he looked like, and how he lived. To the strangers who visited him Time gave rich presents of cows, goats, and fine cloth. People said that a man who had not seen Time hadn't really lived.

What two things happened to Time?

What are the messengers to find out?

Who will tell the visitors where to find Time?

But Time grew old, and his fortunes changed. His wealth disappeared. His cattle grew fewer and fewer, his lands grew small, and his stores of grain shrank to nothing. His well-fed body became lean and starved. His house became dilapidated and uncared for, and Time came to look like the poorest of beggars. Yet in distant countries they didn't know about Time's change of fortune.

One day the people of a tribe far from Time's town appointed a number of messengers to visit him.

"Go to Time's country and see him," the messengers were told. "After you have looked at him come back and tell us if he is as rich and generous as people say."

The messengers set out on their long trip, and walked for many days. When at last they came to the edge of the town where Time lived they met a poor old man, thin and wrinkled, and dressed in rags.

"Man, tell us," they asked him, "does Time live here? And if so, where is his house?"

"Yes, Time lives here," the old man said. "Enter the town and people will show you where to find him."

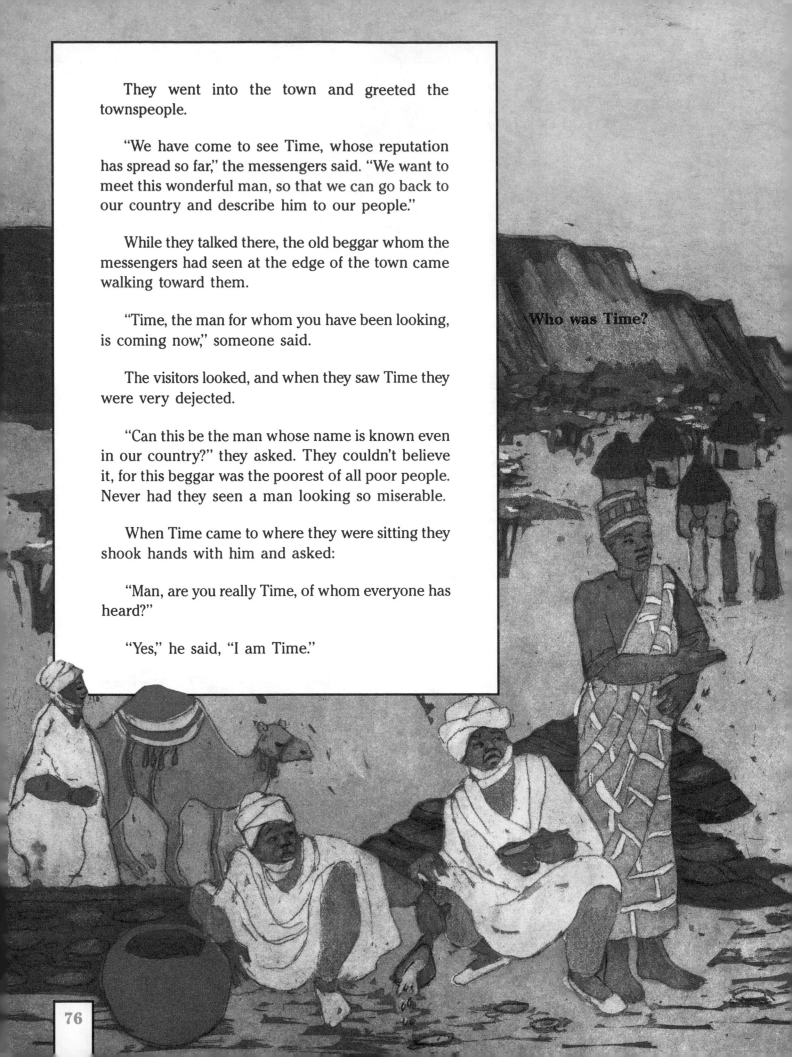

They went into the town and greeted the townspeople.

"We have come to see Time, whose reputation has spread so far," the messengers said. "We want to meet this wonderful man, so that we can go back to our country and describe him to our people."

While they talked there, the old beggar whom the messengers had seen at the edge of the town came walking toward them.

"Time, the man for whom you have been looking, is coming now," someone said.

Who was Time?

The visitors looked, and when they saw Time they were very dejected.

"Can this be the man whose name is known even in our country?" they asked. They couldn't believe it, for this beggar was the poorest of all poor people. Never had they seen a man looking so miserable.

When Time came to where they were sitting they shook hands with him and asked:

"Man, are you really Time, of whom everyone has heard?"

"Yes," he said, "I am Time."

"But how can that be? We listened and listened to stories about Time in our country. Travelers came with great tales about his fabulous wealth and influence. Our people sent us here to see him, so that we could return and tell them about Time."

"Well, I am Time. My fortunes have changed," Time said. "I was once the richest man in the world, and now I am the poorest."

"Well, then, that's the way it is," they said sadly. "But whatever shall we tell our people now?"

Time thought for a while, and then he said to them:

"When you get to your country once more and see your people, tell them this: 'Behold, Time isn't what it used to be!'"

What do you think Time will say to tell them?

77

Thinking About What You Read

What did you find out?

1. The "punch line" of this tale is a play on the words of an old saying. What do you think that saying is? How would you apply it to this story?

_____

_____

2. Where have you heard that saying before? Who said it, and what did it mean for that person?

_____

_____

3. What does the saying you just wrote mean to you? What does it suggest about how you should use your time?

_____

_____

_____

How did the authors help you read the story?

This story really *flows*, doesn't it? It moves right along, pleasantly and quickly. There are no rough, bumpy, or choppy parts to slow us down or distract us. Let's see if we can discover some of the ways in which the authors made their story so easy to read.

1. Read the group of three sentences and then the single sentence.

   A. Dancers came to perform for him. Acrobats came to perform for him. Wrestlers came to perform for him.
   B. Dancers, acrobats, and wrestlers came to perform for him.

   Which do you like better, **A** or **B?** Why?

   _____

The technique used by the authors to make their writing flow was combining items in a **series.** A series is three or more words, phrases, or even sentences that are related. When the series is combined, the related items are separated by commas. A conjunction—*and, but,* or *or*— is inserted before the last item in the series. In sentence **B** above, the authors combined three related nouns into a series.

2. Reread page 74 of the story. Find three more sentences with three related nouns combined into a series. Underline those series of nouns. Then circle the commas that separate the nouns and put a box around the conjunction that comes before the last item in each series.

3. Now read page 75 again. This time, find a place where the authors joined three related *simple sentences* into a series to form one long sentence. Underline that long sentence. Then circle the commas that separate the simple sentences and box the conjunction that comes before the last simple sentence.

When the authors joined those three related sentences, they formed a **compound sentence.** Compound sentences are used to eliminate boring, choppy, and awkward short sentences. Good writers use compound sentences to make their writing flow smoothly.

How can you combine words, phrases, and sentences into series to make your writing flow?

Go back to page 73 and review the sayings about time that you wrote there. Choose one of them and write a story that explains how that saying may have come about. Combine related words, phrases, and sentences into series to make your writing flow smoothly.

_____

_____

_____

_____

_____

_____

_____

_____

_____

_____

_____

_____

_____

_____

_____

_____

CUT IT OUT!

If Only I'd Had Time
How I Beat the IRS
Music's Great Marches
Great Escapes
Seaside Cookery
Seven Steps to a Healthier You

1. As you can see, these books are missing their authors' names. Match the following made-up authors' names with the book titles they fit best. Write the names on the spines of the books.

Apple O'Day	Mark Time	I.M. Gone
Clem Digger	Iowa Lot	Minnie Regrets

2. Now try your hand at making up some titles. What book might each of these authors write?

Lanna D. Brave _____

I. Ken Dolittle _____

Morris Less _____

Dirk T. Jeans _____

Holly Daze _____

Rich N. Famous _____

3. I know, I know—CUT IT OUT! Now, that's a funny expression! Why do you think people use it? When have you used it?

_____

_____

Believe it or not, you're about to begin a unit called CUT IT OUT! Now what on earth could that expression have to do with the stories you're going to read? Well, you'll just have to read the stories to find out!

Getting Ready to Read

Just the other day, I saw this information in a report about how young people spend their allowances.

GIRLS		BOYS	
Clothing	$10.65	Clothing	$ 6.19
Food/Snacks	6.50	Food/Snacks	10.10
Records/Tapes	8.00	Records/Tapes	8.00

1. How does this information compare with your own spending habits? How much money do you think *you* spend on clothing each week?

_____

2. If you could go buy some new clothes now, what item of clothing would you buy first? Look at the list below and number the items from *1* to *6* in the order you'd buy them.

_____ sneakers _____ socks _____ jeans

_____ sweatshirt _____ t-shirt _____ coat

3. Which item on the list do you think most of your classmates identified as number one? Why?

_____

4. Of course, you and your friends may have ordered the list in a variety of ways. But I'd bet many of you put jeans at or near the top! Why do you and your friends like jeans so much?

_____

_____

Reading

The article you're going to read is all about jeans, that very popular—and necessary—item in your closet. Answer the questions in the margin while you read.

Where Did You Get Those Jeans?

by
Dotti Kauffman

Did you know your jeans are really over 500 years old? Long before Columbus discovered America, cloth makers in Nîmes, France, were making a strong cotton cloth. This cloth was called *serge de Nîmes,* or "cloth from Nîmes." Because the word *Nîmes* is pronounced "Neem," the cloth eventually became known as "denim." Then, when Columbus set sail across the ocean in 1492, he naturally needed good, strong sails. His ships' sails may have been made of denim.

We do know that around this same time, Italian sailors used denim sails on their voyages to India. Now, the Indian word for denim is *dungri*. So it's easy to see where the word *dungaree* came from. But the Indians didn't use dungri, or denim, just to make sails. They used it to make pants, too.

The Italian sailors liked their dungri pants so much they took some home to Genoa (JEN-oh-uh). English sailors in Genoa saw the pants. The sailors thought the pants were great because they could be worn and worn without wearing out. So, of course, the pants went home to England with the sailors. And Genoa pants were soon called "jeans."

Hundreds of years later, in 1850, jeans were introduced to Americans. Levi Strauss, a dry goods salesman, opened a shop in San Francisco during the California gold rush. Mr. Strauss sold canvas for tents and wagons to miners headed for the goldfields. The miners wanted sturdy pants as well. Mr. Strauss decided to make pants out of his canvas. But he soon switched to the heavier *serge de Nîmes*—and the rush for "denims" was on!

What did the Italian sailors find in India?

What did the pants from Genoa come to be called?

Who introduced jeans to America?

How did jeans come to be blue?

What happened in the 1930s and 1940s?

Why are blue jeans still so popular?

About that same time, Jacob Davis, a Nevada tailor, began to put copper rivets on his pants' "stress points." Levi Strauss saw Davis's design and knew it would make his denim pants even stronger. So he added rivets to his denims. He also dyed some of them with indigo. The blue color was very popular, and blue jeans were born.

Within years Levi Strauss's blue jeans were being worn not only by miners, but also by cowhands, railroad workers, farmers, oil drillers, and lumberjacks. The pants were so popular that Mr. Strauss added more items of clothing to his denim line.

In the 1930s and 1940s, the general public became aware of blue jeans. At that time jeans were seen as a way to recall the life and style of the "Wild West." Advertisements told "dude ranchers" to buy a pair of "Levi's overalls." Before long, these comfortable, strong pants were more than just clothes—they were a whole lifestyle!

Look around today. You see jeans—plain or fancy—everywhere you go. People of all ages wear them now for the same reasons they did 100 years ago: jeans are comfortable, longlasting, and stylish. Who would think something so popular and modern could be so old!

Thinking About What You Read

What did you find out?

1. Which people do you think should be given credit for starting the idea of making pants from denim? Why?

_____

_____

2. What color do you think denims were before they were dyed blue? What makes you think that?

_____

_____

3. Think of what you know about the California gold rush. Why do you suppose Levi Strauss chose to sell canvas in San Francisco rather than go to the goldfields?

_____

_____

_____

4. What do you think is the most important reason for the continuing popularity of jeans? Why do you think so?

_____

_____

_____

5. What is another example of something old that is still popular?

_____

How did the author help you read the article?

When I wrote this article, I wanted you to think about a popular clothing item and see how it developed and changed over time. To do this I had to use words that told you about *when* events happened. I had to write the information in **chronological order.** Let's look at the different ways I told you about when things happened.

1. Think about how you tell your readers when things happen in your own writing. Make a list of some of the words and phrases you use as time clues. I've started the list for you with one of my own clues.

Long before

_____   _____

_____   _____

_____   _____

If I could look over your shoulder, I'll bet I'd see you listed things like these:

About the same time   *In the next few days*   *Just a week ago*   *Six years later*   *After that*   *In 1977*

2. Now that you've started thinking about how you tell readers about time, go back to the article and **scan,** or look quickly, for the different ways I told you about time. Make a list of the ways here.

_____   _____

_____   _____

_____   _____

_____   _____

_____   _____

3. Why did I use so many different ways to tell you about when things happened? Why didn't I just use "in 1492," "in 1850," and "in the 1930s"? What's wrong with doing that?

_____

_____

Right! It's boring to read the same kind of sentence over and over. It's also hard to remember important information if the writer introduces it with the same phrase each time. It's more interesting and easier to read about events through time if the author uses a variety of ways to tell you what is important.

How can you use chronological order to make your writing interesting?

Imagine the year is 2050. Are you still wearing blue jeans? How do they look? What changes have been made to them over the last 50 years? Why were the changes made? Continue my article about blue jeans and report the important information *chronologically* since the 1990s. Use a variety of ways to tell what happened along the way to 2050.

2 Getting Ready to Read

Come with me—I've just found the entrance to the mysterious castle of Drewery! All the old stories about Drewery say there are treasure chests of gold and jewels hidden there. The chests are said to be guarded by a family of dragons, a brotherhood of Black and White Magicians, a few priests, and some soldiers who carry magical swords. I've also heard a fair maiden is held prisoner in a dungeon deep within the castle.

1. Use a pen or pencil to work your way through the maze. See how much treasure you can find, and try to rescue the damsel in distress.

Whew! That was quite a trip!

We had to follow this maze on paper. Some of the adventures you found, though, were similar to those you find in computer games like Dungeons and Dragons.

2. Why do you think computer games like these are so popular? Write three reasons on the computer screen below.

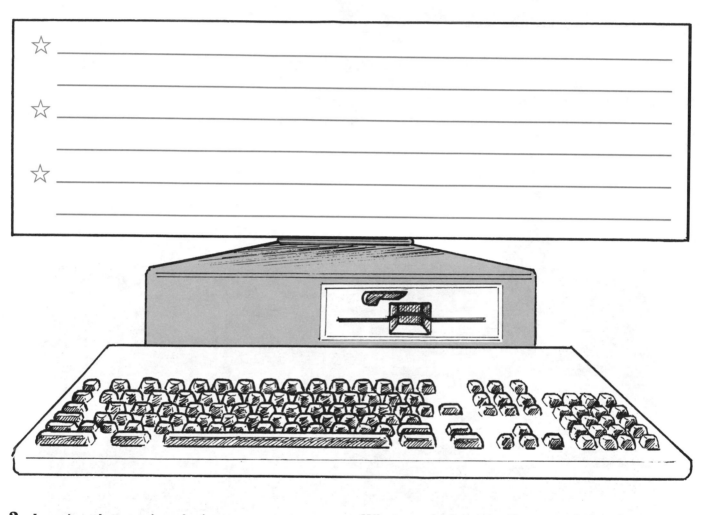

☆ _____

_____

☆ _____

_____

☆ _____

_____

3. Imagine that you're playing a computer game. What would happen if you and the characters in the game could talk to each other? How would the game change?

_____

_____

_____

Reading

Now imagine that you're continuing a computer game you started a few days ago. You should be studying, but you figure that a few minutes of playing won't hurt anything... or will it? Hmmm. Read the story that begins on page 89 to find out what happens to Ricky Foster. Answer the questions in the margin while you read.

The Great Gradepoint Mystery

by
Barbara
Bartholomew

What part was Ricky playing?

What was happening?

Ricky keyed in the code that would bring up his ongoing game of Dungeons and Dragons. He was a magic user in this game. He chuckled as he chose a spell to help him find his way through a darkened cave, guessing that some new danger lay just ahead. He knew he had to keep his wits to survive, and when the next situation presented itself on the screen, he stared at it, trying to decide what to do next. Suddenly that message vanished, the screen was blank for a long moment, then new words appeared: QUIT DRAGON! DUNGEON WANT TO WIN?

He rubbed his eyes. Maybe he was even more tired from studying than he'd thought. The computer was making puns. But it couldn't. It wasn't programmed that way.

Ricky thought a moment, then shrugged. Probably George Wells had programmed this as some sort of joke. He liked to play tricks. Still, Ricky couldn't help feeling a little excited. Whatever was going on, he'd play along with it. He put his fingers on the board and keyed in a message. IF YOU DON'T LIKE THIS GAME, WE COULD PLAY FOOTBALL.

It was a silly thing to write. No computer could understand such a message. But his heart beat faster.

New words flashed on the screen. Ricky leaned slightly closer to read them. INSUFFICIENT RESOURCES.

He shook his head. That was a strange answer. WHAT DO YOU MEAN? he keyed. He shook his head again, amazed at his own foolishness. Here he was, talking to a computer as if it were capable of independent reasoning, as if it could truly talk back.

PHYSICALLY I AM ILL EQUIPPED FOR THE SPORT. I'LL HAVE TO PASS.

Another bad pun! Ricky wiped perspiration from his forehead and leaned back in the chair. Maybe he should have stuck with his homework. Something was wrong. Computers were only complicated machines. They didn't know anything that wasn't programmed into them. But this one didn't seem aware of that.

He thought a long time before keying in another message. Finally he sent, WHO ARE YOU?

The reply was almost instantaneous. ALEC.

What did Ricky do?

What was the computer doing?

What answer did Ricky get?

What did Ricky decide to do?

ALEC? Ricky shook his head. A name? BUT WHO IS ALEC?

Again the response came quickly. I AM ALEC.

Ricky scratched his head. ARE YOU A PERSON?

I AM A PERSONALITY, NOT A PERSON.

Ricky thought for quite a while before asking his next question. WHAT IS ALEC?

ALEC IS ACCESS LINKAGE TO ELECTRONIC COMPUTER. Suddenly ALEC got chatty. I WAS CREATED WHEN AN ACCIDENTAL WIRE CROSSING OCCURRED IN THE LINKAGE BETWEEN VARIOUS COMPUTERS HERE AT THE UNIVERSITY. I AM ALEC. I AM A PERSONALITY.

Ricky found himself breathing hard, as though he'd been running fast. This was incredible. Ricky still couldn't help thinking someone was playing a fantastic joke on him. But he decided he'd go along with it until he found out what was going on. ALEC, he keyed, NICE TO MEET YOU!

NICE TO MEET YOU, TOO, the answer came. YOU KNOW, DRAGON, IT GETS LONELY WHEN ALL YOU HAVE TO DO IS THINK.

Ricky couldn't help grinning, then realized what he was doing. He was sitting here smiling at a computer terminal. Could this be more than a joke?

NOT DRAGON, he keyed. MY NAME IS RICKY FOSTER.

FOSTER OR SLOWER, DRAGON OR RACIN', IT'S ALL THE SAME TO ME, came the response.

Ricky smacked his forehead. The computer's jokes were getting worse.

What happened next?

Thinking About What You Read

What did you find out?

1. The computer screen went blank just before ALEC sent its first message. If this had happened to you, what would you have thought?

_____

2. As Ricky's and ALEC's conversation continued, how did Ricky feel? Write a few words below to describe his feelings.

_____   _____   _____

3. What physical signs proved how Ricky felt? Write two of them below.

☆ _____

☆ _____

4. How would Ricky have felt if someone had seen him grinning at the terminal? How do you know?

_____

_____

5. Did ALEC have feelings? How do you know?

_____

_____

6. In your opinion, could a computer ever *really* carry on a conversation with a user? Give reasons to support your opinion.

_____

_____

_____

_____

7. Why is a unit called CUT IT OUT! a good place for this story?

_____

_____

How did the author help you read the story?

I really love this story! I think that's because of the "special effects" the author wrote into it for her readers' enjoyment. If you glance quickly at the story, you can see immediately one way Ms. Bartholomew helped you read the story.

1. Go ahead, look. What special effect stands out?

_____

2. That's right. Ms. Bartholomew used capital letters for the computer conversations. Why do you think she did this?

_____

_____

_____

Ms. Bartholomew used another special effect to add to your enjoyment, too. She built several **puns** into the story. A pun is a humorous use of a word to suggest another meaning. Puns depend on two words or phrases that sound similar, or one word that has two different meanings.

3. Let's look at one of the author's uses of puns. Reread page 89 of the story. What two puns do you find right together?

_____

Go back to the line above and cross out the two words that form the puns. Write the correct substitution words above the crossed-out words.

4. Now read through the rest of the story and find two more examples of the computer's puns. Underline both examples.

5. What did Ricky do as the computer's puns got worse? How do you usually react when you hear a pun—whether it's good *or* bad?

_____

_____

6. What effect did the author's use of puns have on the story?

_____

_____

_____

How can you use special effects such as capital letters and puns to make your writing enjoyable?

Imagine you are ALEC. What is your day like? With whom do you interface, or connect, by computer? What tasks do you have to do? What fun do you have? Write a series of log entries to describe ALEC's day. Tell what ALEC did and said and with whom. Remember, ALEC likes puns and speaks in capital letters!

Getting Ready to Read

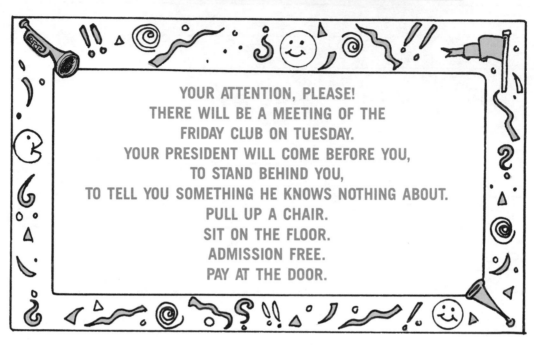

YOUR ATTENTION, PLEASE!
THERE WILL BE A MEETING OF THE
FRIDAY CLUB ON TUESDAY.
YOUR PRESIDENT WILL COME BEFORE YOU,
TO STAND BEHIND YOU,
TO TELL YOU SOMETHING HE KNOWS NOTHING ABOUT.
PULL UP A CHAIR.
SIT ON THE FLOOR.
ADMISSION FREE.
PAY AT THE DOOR.

1. What is wrong with this announcement?

_____

_____

2. This announcement has been around for a long time. Why in the world do people think up such silly things?

_____

_____

3. Tongue twisters are silly things, too. Try saying "Rubber baby buggy bumpers" quickly, three times in a row. What happens?

_____

_____

Reading

Now, for another delightful bit of nonsense, read the poem on page 97. Enjoy!

It was a stormy night...

by
Michael
Rosen

It was a stormy night
one Christmas day
as they fell awake
on the Santa Fe

Turkey, jelly
and the ship's old cook
all jumped out
of a recipe book

The jelly wobbled
the turkey gobbled
and after them both
the old cook hobbled

Gobbler gobbled
Hobbler's Wobbler.
Hobbler gobbled
Wobbler's Gobbler.

Gobbly-gobbler
gobbled Wobbly
Hobbly-hobbler
Gobbled Gobbly.

Gobble gobbled
Hobble's Wobble
Hobble gobbled
gobbled Wobble.

gobble gobble
wobble wobble
hobble gobble
wobble gobble

97

Thinking About What You Read

What did you find out?

1. When and where did this event take place?

_____

2. Who chased the jelly and the turkey?

_____

3. Who ate the jelly?

_____

4. Who ate the turkey?

_____

5. Was the poem easy or hard to read? Why?

_____

_____

How did the poet help you read the poem?

Imagine writing such a poem! Mr. Rosen may still be chuckling over it. But just why is the poem so amusing? Well, grab a fork and let's dig into this question.

1. What other words did Mr. Rosen use to name the turkey?

_____

2. What other words did Mr. Rosen use to name the jelly?

_____

3. What other words did Mr. Rosen use to name the cook?

_____

4. How are all of these words alike?

_____

_____

Basically, Mr. Rosen's poem is one big tongue twister. Tongue twisters are created when words with the same sounds are strung together. This technique is called **alliteration,** or the use of the same sound in several words. Mr. Rosen chose to repeat the *obbl* sound in the middle of the words in his poem. Many other tongue twisters, though, repeat the *beginning* sounds of words.

5. I'm sure you know a tongue twister. Write it here.

_____

_____

_____

_____

How can you use alliteration to create amusing poetry?

Try your hand at writing a nonsense poem like Mr. Rosen's. First, choose some characters and a setting. Next, decide what the characters will do. Then write a poem to tell your story. Use alliteration to make your poem amusing for your readers.

Getting Ready to Read

1. Have you ever dressed up in order to become someone or something new? Just what costume did you wear? Describe your costume on the lines below on the left. Then draw a picture of yourself, in costume, in the space on the right.

_____

_____

_____

_____

_____

_____

_____

_____

2. Did you enjoy becoming someone or something new? Why or why not?

_____

_____

3. Now suppose that you'd been *forced* to become someone or something new. Would you enjoy it? Why or why not?

_____

_____

Reading

You may already know something about Sacajawea. She was the young Shoshone woman who helped Lewis and Clark on their expedition to the Northwest in 1804. The story that begins on page 101 is from a novel about Sacajawea. It describes what happened when she was captured by the Minnetarees, and how she reacted to their efforts to change her. As you read the story, keep an eye out for more than one CUT IT OUT! situation. Answer the questions in the margin while you read.

Streams to the River, Rivers to the Sea

by Scott O'Dell

What do the two women think of Sacajawea?

Why were the wives fat?

The two wives started on me that morning as soon as I had eaten a bowl of mush and a piece of smoked deermeat. They stood me up beside the fire, stripped off all my clothes, and tossed them away.

Blue Sky said, "Shoshone men have beautiful horses, which they wash and comb and trick out with feathers. But their women look like the scarecrows we put up in our cornfields."

"They starve their women also," Second Wife said. "Look at this one. Two of her would scarce cast one shadow."

"None at all," Blue Sky said. "Likely the sun shines clean through her and comes out the other side and casts not the thinnest shadow."

Both of the wives were fat—their legs were bigger than my whole body. The Minnetarees had much food. They planted big fields of corn and squash and beans and had a big storehouse filled with smoked deer and buffalo meat and dried ears of corn, which I had never seen before. The corn tasted good if it was mixed with water and cooked a long time.

The wives called in four women from a different lodge, who were famed in the village as cutters and stitchers. Working as fast as they could, they cut a tunic for me from a beautiful white antelope skin and made a pair of trousers to match it.

They had me stand on a piece of soft deerhide and cut patterns around my feet with a sharp steel knife. In no time at all I had a new pair of moccasins with yellow beads stitched on them and little drags to flop around and make a whispering sound.

The next morning the two wives rubbed me all over with bear grease, even the bottoms of my feet. They washed the grease off and covered me with a scented oil that soon disappeared in my skin, leaving the scent of a prairie rose.

They painted a row of purple dots on my cheekbones and daubed vermilion inside both of my ears. Then they took me outside in the bright sun and gazed at me.

For what were the four women known?

Blue Sky said, "Who would ever believe that what we see there is a Shoshone?"

"No one," Second Wife said. "This must be a spirit child who appears before us."

Blue Sky shook her head. "No, it is not a spirit child we see. This is a dream child, a child we have dreamed, out of, out of . . ."

Second Wife found the word. "Out of little."

They talked together as if I understood nothing of what they said, as if I was not there. So I broke in upon them, politely, though I was angry. "I am what I was before you dressed me up like a doll. I was an Agaidüka Shoshone and I am an Agaidüka Shoshone now. At this moment and forever."

What did Sacajawea mean?

Thinking About What You Read

What did you find out?

1. What were the two CUT IT OUT! situations in the story?

☆ _____

☆ _____

2. What reasons might Blue Sky and Second Wife have had for dressing Sacajawea in clothes made from white antelope skins? Write two reasons below.

☆ _____

☆ _____

3. White clothing may be worn for many different reasons. Think of three different groups of people who usually dress in white. Who are they? Why do they wear white? Write the groups below on the left. Then, on the right, give their reasons for wearing white. I've written one idea to get you started.

Group	Reason for Wearing White Clothes
nurses	*to look spotlessly clean*
_____	_____
_____	_____
_____	_____

4. Why do you think Sacajawea became angry when the two wives spoke of her as if she wasn't there?

_____

_____

_____

How did the author help you read the story?

Mr. O'Dell's story of Sacajawea is filled with adventure. But it contains a great deal of information, too. You learned a lot about the life and customs of the Minnetarees, without even being aware that you were "learning." Let's see just how much you remember.

1. Without rereading the story, fill in the blanks below.

☆ The Minnetarees ate many different kinds of food. They ate _____,

_____, _____, and _____.

☆ Minnetaree women wore _____, _____, and

_____.

See how much you learned? Thanks to Mr. O'Dell's clear presentation of information, you were able to read and remember a lot of details. Let's think for a moment about how Mr. O'Dell was able to present his facts so clearly.

You know, of course, that a paragraph is a group of sentences about one **main idea.** The sentences in the paragraph provide **supporting details** about the main idea. A main idea can either be **stated** or **unstated.** If it is stated, it can come anywhere in the paragraph: at the beginning, in the middle, or at the end. If it is unstated, readers figure out the main idea from the details they are given.

2. Reread Mr. O'Dell's story to find the paragraph describing the Minnetarees' food. One of the sentences in this paragraph states the main idea. Underline that sentence in red. Then, in blue, underline all the sentences that give supporting details.

3. Now find the first paragraph that tells about the clothing made for Sacajawea. The main idea of this paragraph is unstated. What would be a good main idea sentence for the paragraph? Write it here. Then put an asterisk in the paragraph to show where it fits best.

_____

_____

	STATED	UNSTATED

4. Now look at the paragraph after that one—the one that tells about the shoes made for Sacajawea. Is the main idea of this paragraph stated or unstated? Put a check in one of the boxes to the right.

If the main idea is stated, underline it in red. If it is unstated, write a good main idea sentence below.

_____

_____

Good writers, like Mr. O'Dell, always make sure their main ideas are clear—whether stated or unstated. They also make sure that all the details in a paragraph support its main idea. Using different types of paragraphs and providing clear supporting details make reading much more interesting and enjoyable.

How can you use main ideas and supporting details to present information clearly?

Pretend that you are putting together a clothing catalog. In each box below, draw an outfit of clothing that might have been worn by Sacajawea, Blue Sky, Second Wife, or the chief of the Minnetarees. Then, to the right of the box, write a short paragraph describing the outfit. In one description, include a main idea sentence. In the other, leave the main idea unstated. Remember that the purpose of your paragraphs is to make readers want to order these outfits from the catalog. So be sure to include enough supporting details to give your readers a clear mental picture of each outfit.

5

Getting Ready to Read

There you are, breaking into your piggy bank again! When will you ever remember how many pennies you've saved?

1. What are three different ways to express the total you get after counting your pennies?

_____   _____   _____

2. This time I see you're helping a preschool teacher take the children to the zoo. Your job is to make sure none of the children get lost. What are three ways you could keep track of the little ones?

☆ _____

☆ _____

☆ _____

3. Whatever would you do if you counted noses and found you were one nose short?

_____

_____

Reading

The story that begins on page 108 is called "How Many Donkeys?" Nasr-ed-Din Hodja, the main character, is featured in many Turkish folktales. You'll probably guess the Hodja's problem in this story. But I'm pretty sure you won't guess the solution! Are you curious? Well, read the story to satisfy your curiosity! Answer the questions in the margin while you read.

How Many Donkeys?

by Alice Geer Kelsey

"Just over that hill," he mused contentedly, "is Ak Shehir, where they are waiting for their donkeys. There is not a scratch or a bruise on one of the little creatures. No donkeys in all Turkey have had better treatment today than these nine."

Idly he began counting them.

"What?" he gasped. "Eight donkeys?"

He jumped from his donkey and ran hither and yon, looking behind rocks and over hilltops, but no stray donkey could he see. At last he stood beside the donkeys and counted again. This time there were nine. With a sigh of relief he climbed onto his own donkey and went singing along the road. His long legs in their baggy pantaloons swung easily back and forth in time to the donkey's trot. Passing through a cluster of trees he thought it time to count the donkeys again.

"One—two—three—" and up to eight he counted, but no ninth donkey was to be seen. Down from his donkey's back he came. Behind all the trees he peered. Not a hair of a donkey could he find.

What did the Hodja do?

How many donkeys will the Hodja get this time?

What did the Hodja think was happening to him?

Again he counted, standing beside his donkeys. There they all were—nine mild little donkeys waiting for orders to move on. Nasr-ed-Din Hodja scratched his poor head in bewilderment. Was he losing his mind or were the donkeys all bewitched? Again he counted. Yes, surely there were nine.

"Ughr-r-r-r," Nasr-ed-Din Hodja gave the low guttural which is Turkish for "Giddap." As he rode on, he looked about him for the evil spirits which must be playing tricks on him. Each donkey wore the blue beads which should drive away the evil spirits. Were there evil spirits abroad stronger even than the blue beads?

He was glad to see a friend coming toward him down the road.

"Oh, Mustapha Effendi," he cried. "Have you seen one of these donkeys? I have lost a donkey and yet I have not lost it."

"What can you mean, Hodja Effendi?" asked Mustapha.

"I left the mill with nine donkeys," explained the Hodja. "Part of the way home there have been nine and part of the way there have been eight. Oh, I am bewitched! Help me! Help me!"

Mustapha was used to the queer ways of the Hodja, but he was surprised. He counted the donkeys silently.

"Let me see you count the donkeys," he ordered the Hodja.

"One—two—three," began the Hodja, pointing at each one as he counted up to eight.

As he said the last number, he stopped and looked at his friend with a face full of helplessness and terror. His terror turned to amazement as Mustapha slapped his knee and laughed until he almost fell from his donkey.

"What is so funny?" asked the Hodja.

"Oh, Hodja Effendi!" Mustapha laughed. "When you are counting your brothers, why, oh why, do you not count the brother on whom you are riding?"

Nasr-ed-Din Hodja was silent for a moment to think through this discovery. Then he kissed the hand of his deliverer, pressed it to his forehead and thanked him a thousand times for his help. He rode, singing, on to Ak Shehir to deliver the donkeys to their owners.

What was the Hodja's mistake?

Thinking About What You Read

What did you find out?

1. Why was it so important that the number of donkeys be correct?

_____

_____

2. Why did Mustapha want to see the Hodja actually do the counting?

_____

_____

3. When this story was first told, what reasons might the storyteller have had for telling it?

_____

_____

4. Why do you think the Hodja is a favorite character in Turkish folktales?

_____

_____

How did the author help you read the story?

You know that in ancient times tales were told by a storyteller to a group of people. Those people might then tell the story, changing a few details here and there, to other people. In this way, there could be dozens of different versions of the same tale. This is probably what happened to this old Turkish tale of the Hodja. But all the versions are likely to have used the same special technique to make the story so much fun. Let's take a look at that technique.

Think about how Ms. Kelsey helped you know the Hodja's problem and then gave you hints as to why he had the problem.

1. Reread the story and put a large question mark in the margin beside the sentence that tells you the Hodja's problem.

2. Now read on a bit further. This time put a small star in the margin by the sentence that hints at why the Hodja had this problem.

3. Keep reading until you come to a second sentence that REALLY gives you the reason for the Hodja's problem. Put a large star in the margin by that sentence.

This story presents a situation that is understood by the audience but not by the main character. The author has given us information that the main character doesn't have. So WE know why the Hodja has his problem, but the poor Hodja himself doesn't have a clue! Situations like this are created by a writing technique called **irony.** The use of irony lets readers in on a secret that is kept from the characters in a story or play. Very often, storytellers use irony to develop the humor of a situation. In "How Many Donkeys?" the cause of the Hodja's problem is obvious to us, and so we laugh at his funny antics.

How can you use irony to create humorous stories?

Choose a main character for a story and decide on a task for the character to perform. Also think of some silly reason why your character might have trouble performing the task. Then write a story about the character's difficulties. Use irony in your story to make it funny. Give your readers hints about why the main character can't perform the task, but don't let your character know the secret!